Imagineers Impresarios Inventors

Imagineers Impresarios Inventors

Cincinnati's Arts and the Power of Her

Edited by Kathy Merchant

Orange *frazer* Press

Wilmington, Ohio

ISBN 978-1949248-173
Copyright©2020 Cincinnati Institute of Fine Arts dba ArtsWave
All Rights Reserved

Published for ArtsWave by:
Orange Frazer Press
37½ West Main St.
P.O. Box 214
Wilmington, OH 45177

For price and shipping information, call: 937.382.3196
Or visit: www.orangefrazer.com

Book and cover design by: Kelly Schutte and Orange Frazer Press

Library of Congress Control Number: 2020902671

First Printing
Printed in China

CINCINNATI OPERA'S 2007 PRODUCTION OF GIUSEPPE VERDI'S "AIDA"

CINCINNATI BALLET "NUTCRACKER" (2017)

CONTENTS

NRITYARPANA

SPONSORS

Our thanks and gratitude to those who made this project possible.

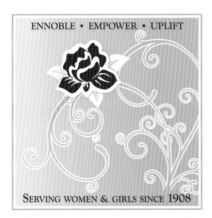

BOOK SPONSORS

Karen Bowman
Melanie M. Chavez
Carol Ann and Ralph V. Haile, Jr. / U.S. Bank Foundation
Landen Family Foundation
Sara M. and Michelle Vance Waddell
The Women's Fund of Greater Cincinnati Foundation

POWER OF HER SPONSORS

Procter & Gamble
Charlotte Schmidlapp Fund, Fifth Third Bank, Trustee

ENSEMBLE THEATRE CINCINNATI "RIPCORD" (2019)

ACKNOWLEDGMENTS

WITH SPECIAL GRATITUDE FROM

arts wave

Funding Arts. Fueling Community.

We all have this book to enjoy, and the opportunity to get to know many of the incredible women who have shaped our community's cultural vibrancy, thanks to the people who inspired this publication with great enthusiasm. In addition to the story writers, photographers, and our sponsors, ArtsWave wishes to acknowledge:

Kathy Merchant, Managing Director and Editor, for her vision and dedication to bring this publication to light and life.

Patty Beggs, Chairperson, for leading our arts organizations in creation of an 18-month community-wide celebration of the Power of Her.

LPK, for the creative design of the Power of Her brand.

Cincinnati Art Museum and **Cincinnati Museum Center,** for background research to identify often-overlooked legacy leaders.

Cincinnati's Arts Organizations, for supplying content and photos.

Jeff Suess (*Cincinnati Enquirer*), **John Fox** (*Cincinnati Magazine*), **Kevin Cox** (*Cincinnati Business Courier*), and **Beth Sullebarger** (preservation consultant), for their assistance in obtaining quality historical images and citations.

Robin Lippelman, Art Academy of Cincinnati, for her diligent volunteer role as fact-checker and content/style editor for the entire publication.

ArtsWave Staff: Project Manager Krista Bondi, for her diligent design and technology work behind the scenes, and Vice President Lisa Wolter for her wise counsel throughout the process.

ArtsWave Leadership:
Community Campaign Chairs: Jill McGruder (2020), Jill Meyer (2016) and Melanie Healey (2014) for their support and advocacy for the arts. Melanie Healey, who founded the Women's Leadership Roundtable. Past Board Chairs: Teresa Tanner, Lisa Sauer, and Karen Bowman for their leadership of the organization's sustainable future.

And a collective "thank you" to everyone in our community who nominated leading women, and who reviewed the nominations for the amazing women in this book!

CINCINNATI PLAYHOUSE IN THE PARK

FOREWORD

One hundred years ago, the 19th amendment to the U.S. Constitution was ratified, giving women the right to vote. One hundred years before that, a time of great social activism led to local calls for civic reform.

Women sustained prominent roles in these local movements for a century, uniting nationally in 1848 at the Seneca Falls Convention, and launching the women's suffrage movement two decades later. While details are sparse about the roles of Cincinnati women leading up to 1920, Ohio was the fifth state to ratify the constitutional amendment, and Cincinnati created one of the oldest chapters of the national League of Women Voters.

Emboldened by this blossoming of civic activism, groups of Cincinnati women turned their attention to cultivating the community's arts and culture in the early 1850s. We might think of them as our earliest collaborators. They started enduring institutions, and inspired generations of individual artists.

Sarah Worthington King Peter founded the Ladies Academy of Fine Arts in 1854 to encourage interest in producing and appreciating art and music. She is credited with laying the groundwork for what became the Art Academy of Cincinnati in 1869. In 1877, Elizabeth Williams Perry (and many women from the Ladies Academy) founded the Women's Art Museum Association, paving the way for the Cincinnati Art Museum in 1886. Harriet Beecher Stowe, who lived through most of this activist period, was a leader in the abolitionist movement and the renowned author of *Uncle Tom's Cabin* (1852) which continues to inspire debate today. Four enduring organizations were founded in the late 1800s: Cincinnati May Festival, Cincinnati Symphony Orchestra, University of Cincinnati College-Conservatory of Music, and the Woman's Art Club.

This creative imperative and strong leadership gained momentum throughout the 20th century. Cincinnati Opera and the Junior League of Cincinnati are celebrating centennial anniversaries in 2020. During 1920–40, the Cincinnati region was blessed with creation of the Baker Hunt Arts & Cultural Center, Contemporary Arts Center, and Taft Museum of Art. The Cincinnati Institute of Fine Arts (now ArtsWave) was born from one of the nation's first community challenges—by Anna Sinton Taft and her husband Charles—to pool financial resources to support the arts. Fifteen more women-led organizations, all featured in this book, were established between 1950 and 2000.

Standing on the shoulders of women who came before them, the next generation of arts leaders have accelerated the pace of innovation. In the first two decades of the 21st century, women have founded at least nine diverse new arts organizations. The wave continues.

What is most remarkable about this short preview of Cincinnati's leading women in the arts is the sustainability of the organizations they created over a period of 170 years. Though many may say there have been moments of rough sledding to support fresh relevance across changing times, the journey has clearly been worth it.

We hope you will enjoy reading the 120 essays in this book featuring some of the legacy and contemporary imagineers, impresarios, and inventors (and their collaborators) whose "Power of Her" has shaped our community's cultural vibrancy. They, along with scores of colleagues and women who lead corporate and foundation philanthropy, have significantly enhanced the quality of our lives and the character of our region.

This is just the first act. It is certain that Cincinnati's women in the arts will continue to innovate and create for the next century and beyond.

—Alecia Kintner
President and CEO
ArtsWave

—Kathy Merchant
Managing Director & Editor

Imagineers
Impresarios
Inventors

Chapter One

LEAVING A LEGACY

Georgia Beasley

Rosemary Clooney

Patricia Corbett

Doris Day

Jackie Demaline

Mary Emery

Carol Ann Haile

Edie McKee Harper

Elizabeth "Betty"
   Wohlgemuth Herschede

Mary Ellyn Hutton

Irma Lazarus

Ruth Lyons

Loretta Manggrum

Mary Louise McLaughlin

Louise Nippert

Elizabeth Nourse

Harriet Marsh Page

Norma Petersen

Patricia Renick

Mamie Smith

Harriet Beecher Stowe

Aralee Strange

Anna Sinton Taft

Alice Weston

Phyllis Weston

GEORGIA BEASLEY

1903–2005

When Georgia Beasley returned to the University of Cincinnati (UC) in 2004 at age 101, she did so as the institution's oldest living black alumna. In a ceremony she was dubbed "Queen Mother" by the university's African American Cultural and Research Center.

In various African countries, queen mothers are afforded the utmost respect and deference, and at that point in her life, Beasley had more than earned such accolades.

Born in Lexington, Kentucky, Beasley graduated from UC with a degree in home economics in 1925 before she went on to earn a master's degree in art education from Columbia University. At a time when the social and political climate impeded any grandiose career aspirations a black woman may have had, Beasley was determined to reach her goals. "I knew what I wanted to do and where I wanted to go, and I just did it," she told students, family and friends during that UC ceremony. "If you want to do something just do it!"

Beasley spent the bulk of her adult life educating children in the Cincinnati Public Schools as well as spending the summer months teaching down South. When she wasn't teaching, she sang in the choir at Gaines United Methodist Church, forging relationships with local and national artists and musicians through her work in the arts community, including opera singers Marian Anderson and Kathleen Battle. Beasley studied voice for 15 years under Louis John Johen, who said "she had a love of music along with a lovely soprano voice."

Jim Jones, a founding member of the Donald P. Sowell Committee at the Cincinnati Art Museum, met Beasley through the Cincinnati chapter of Links in the 1980s. "She was a dynamic person," said Jim Jones, also a local archivist who served as the historian for the local chapter of the NAACP for more than 20 years. "She was one of the few women of color who were involved in all of this (change) during that time."

A few years after her death, a relative, Allen J. Beasley of Chicago, Illinois, started the Georgia E. Beasley Scholarship at UC in her honor.

"I was blessed to have black women role models in my life that were educators—one was my mom and another was definitely Mrs. Beasley," said Leisan Smith, Director of Community Engagement for Bexley (Ohio) City Schools, who was the first recipient of the Beasley scholarship in 2006. "Her story and history inspired me and my career trajectory. Knowing what she endured let me know that I could continue to work hard, even when I was in a tough work situation, and continue to succeed. It was always such an honor to be in her presence and hear her tell her story."

In 2003, Beasley was awarded the Art Consortium of Cincinnati's Dreamkeeper Award and Lifetime Achievement Award. She also spent many years as a member of the Symphony's Women's Committee and was elected to the group's Hall of Fame.

—Aiesha D. Little

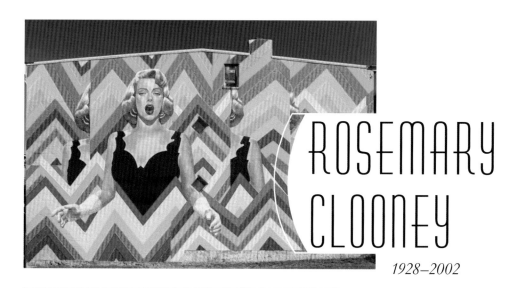

ROSEMARY CLOONEY

1928–2002

Rosemary Clooney's smooth, rich voice radiated through living rooms across America in the 1950s. Jazz was her first love, and she excelled at Big Band swing. Yet, it was novelty hits—nonsensical songs made popular during World War II—that launched her career.

Born in Maysville, Kentucky, it was perhaps Rosemary's difficult childhood that gave her the drive to make it. Her mother traveled for work and eventually divorced an alcoholic husband. She remarried and left the family for California, taking son Nick along. Rosemary and her sister Betty lived with their father, who eventually also left them. She was mostly raised by her grandparents.

Singing was their salve. The sisters performed from the time they were young girls. At 16 and 13, Rosemary and Betty set out alone to pursue their dreams in nearby Cincinnati.

To make ends meet, they collected cans and bottles and sang at local venues. In 1945, they were hired to sing at radio station WLW for $20 a week each. Billed as the Clooney Sisters, they were on air seven nights a week and performed live with Barney Rapp's band at Castle Farm and Netherland Plaza.

A year later, they joined national band leader Tony Pastor. After touring for three years, Betty returned home, and Rosemary headed to New York to launch a solo career with Columbia Records. She became part of the girl singer movement along with Doris Day, Peggy Lee, and Patti Page. Her first hit in 1950, "Beautiful Brown Eyes," sold a respectable 400,000 copies.

Her big break came in 1951. Music arranger Mitch Miller saw in Rosemary an "exuberant personality that could handle the most outlandish songs and arrangements" and convinced her to record "Come On-a My House." To her surprise, she sold one million copies and launched into stardom. Other novelty hits such as "Botch-A-Me" and "Mambo Italiano" separated her from the girl singer pack.

Rosemary appeared on the *Ed Sullivan Show* 16 times from 1949–66. In 1953, she graced the cover of *TIME* magazine—the first singer to do so, female or male. She made her acting debut in 1954 starring in *White Christmas* with Bing Crosby. Two years later, she hosted *The Rosemary Clooney Show*.

Her career on the rise, at 25 she married actor Jose Ferrer. Together they had five children in five years. In the 1960s, they divorced, remarried, and divorced again. By then dealing with addiction to prescription medication, Rosemary suffered a nervous breakdown in 1968.

The road to recovery was long and difficult for her. Son Gabriel Ferrer explained in an interview, "She pulled herself back together and became a different kind of mother…She was less concerned about chasing fame and more interested in her children."

But getting back to work was problematic. Rock & Roll was the rage, marginalizing singers like Rosemary. In 1975, Bing Crosby invited her to tour with him. It was a true second act. She recorded new songs and performed the rest of her life, also continuing her acting career in movies and television. And she found love again with an early sweetheart, Dante DiPaolo.

"The last 20 years of her life were glorious," said Ferrer. NPR noted, "Her comeback solidified her place in jazz history…as one of the greatest interpreters of American song." Rosemary received a Grammy Award for Lifetime Achievement in 2002.

Today, the legacy of Rosemary Clooney lives on through her music, *Tenderly: The Rosemary Clooney Musical*," and two autobiographies.

—Susan Fellows Crabtree

PATRICIA CORBETT
1909–2008

Patricia Barry Corbett was not a quiet philanthropist. She had no interest in anonymity. On Long Island, where she was raised in the early decades of the 20th Century, she pursued the spotlight as a singer on radio and in clubs.

When she came to Cincinnati with her husband and fellow philanthropist J. Ralph in 1932, she quickly involved herself in the area's musical life by studying voice at the College of Music.

The Corbetts came to Cincinnati when Ralph became a marketing consultant for WLW Radio. Later, he founded a company called NuTone, and Patricia—the one with musical savvy—helped develop the distinctive tones of the door chimes that were the centerpiece of the business.

They sold NuTone in 1955 and established the Corbett Foundation, which soon began a 60-year spending spree the likes of which Greater Cincinnati had never seen before.

Patricia—Pat to all who knew her—adored the Cincinnati Opera's performances at the Zoo. She was charmed by the contrast between the company's rustic pavilion and its world-class singers, but she was determined to provide a performing space befitting the caliber of those singers.

In the late 1960s, the foundation earmarked several million dollars to upgrade the aged technical facilities of Music Hall, which became the Opera's home in 1972. It was more than a physical move. It launched the company into the modern age.

Corbett loved everything about show business, especially mixing it up with performers. She counted Beverly Sills and Norman Treigle among her greatest friends. She talked of pianist Vladimir Ashkenazy visiting Cincinnati in 1958 and practicing in the couple's Indian Hill home. (They later moved to Grandin Road.)

She was not, however, a supporter of *every* arts-related project. When a new arts center—the Aronoff Center—was proposed close to the center of downtown, she led the opposition, sitting outside the Hyde Park Kroger gathering signatures on an anti-Aronoff petition. Her fear was that the city would abandon its commitments to Music Hall.

You could see Corbett's interests—and the family name—in many of the foundation's grants: the Corbett Center for the Performing Arts at University of Cincinnati housing the College-Conservatory of Music (CCM), and a pair of theaters, Corbett Auditorium and the Patricia Corbett Theater. There was the Patricia A. Corbett Theater at Northern Kentucky University. And the Corbett Opera Center and Corbett Tower at Music Hall. When the new School for Creative and Performing Arts (SCPA) opened in 2010, its largest performance space was the Corbett Theater. Perhaps the most popular of their endowed structures is the Riverbend performance complex at Coney Island, including the J. Ralph Corbett Pavilion.

At Mrs. Corbett's insistence, many of the foundation's grants were more personal. They might not make the headlines, but they became central to the musical life of the region.

It was Corbett's underwriting that launched a new string program at Northern Kentucky University, as well as funding for several endowed chairs at CCM and the school's J. Ralph Corbett audio production center. One of the foundation's final grants, announced in 2014, six years after Corbett's death, was $500,000 to support a string program at SCPA.

There have been Greater Cincinnati philanthropists who lavished more money on the arts than Patricia and J. Ralph Corbett. But few have matched their enthusiasm or personal passion for the arts they funded. Small wonder that Opera News once referred to Cincinnati as "the city that Corbett built."

—David Lyman

DORIS DAY

1922–2019

Though the minutiae of her early life may seem like trivia questions, her Cincinnati connections and world-class accomplishments run deeper than a footnote. Doris Mary Ann Von Kappelhoff was delivered in Cincinnati on April 3, 1922, by a midwife.

She was born to German immigrant parents when a can of Log Cabin syrup cost 29 cents, today's behemoth grocery chain was a storefront called the Kroger Grocery & Baking Co., and a subway station was being erected on lower Liberty Street.

Her father, Wilhelm, was the organist at St. Mark's Catholic Church in Evanston. He was also a renowned conductor of several singing societies, including the Clifton Heights Society. Day's family home was not far from the church near Xavier University.

Her parents' divorce when she was eight years old created an abrupt upheaval. Day moved from Evanston to College Hill and then to Price Hill where she settled with her mother—a hardcore hillbilly music lover—in an apartment above Welz Tavern, a bar owned by an uncle.

No one knows where "Day" came from, but the Ella Fitzgerald fan took the name after Cincinnati bandleader Barney Rapp told her Kappelhoff was too cumbersome to pronounce or fit on any marquee.

She joined Rapp's band as the requisite girl singer, appearing at his The Sign of the Drum Nightclub on Reading Road in Bond Hill, later joining clarinetist Jimmy James and his Orchestra at the Pavilion Caprice at the Netherland Plaza. She was 16 years old.

Doris Day had talent. She honed that talent and showed up at the right time and at the right place to advance that talent to the next level: Hollywood.

By her early 20s, Doris was a World War II-era favorite, singing a bookend of now-classic anthems—"Que Sera, Sera (Whatever Will Be, Will Be)" and "Sentimental Journey"—cementing her as America's girl-next-door in the minds and hearts of men and women.

She soon broke into films. Among the nearly 40 films in her oeuvre are *Romance on the High Sea* (1948); *Calamity Jane* (1953); *The Man Who Knew Too Much* (1956); *The Pajama Game* (1957); and *It Happened to Jane* (1959).

Starting in 1968, her five-year run of *The Doris Day Show* pioneered women at the helm of talk/variety shows that today is taken for granted. Ellen Degeneres, Oprah, and even Kelly Clarkson have Doris to thank for opening that door.

She's been honored with the Presidential Medal of Freedom, the Cecil B. DeMille Lifetime Achievement Golden Globe Award, American Lifetime Achievement Grammy Award, and a 1960 Academy Award nomination for *Pillow Talk*. Near the Aronoff Center for the Arts, on Walnut between Sixth and Seventh streets, is "Doris Day Way."

As if all that could be too anemic, Doris predated today's animal rights-conscious dog-parents by at least two generations. Her hometown ties and undying love of animals is evident here and around the world. The Doris Day Dog Park at Mount Airy Forest, the Doris Day Animal Foundation, and the League for Animal Welfare are as much a part of her legacy as acting and singing.

Cincinnati gave Doris Day over to the world, and the world is better for our graciousness and hers.

"I could have happily lived my entire life in Cincinnati, married to a proper Cincinnatian, living in a big old Victorian house, raising a brood of offspring," she told her biographer, "but preordination...had other plans for me."

—Kathy Y. Wilson

JACKIE DEMALINE
1950–2018

Whosoever comes after us will certainly wonder: Does art even exist if no one is there to observe, note, deconstruct, criticize or praise it? Because Jackie Demaline did her job as a theater documentarist, those questions will be asked and unequivocally answered.

Since Jackie Demaline is gone, succumbing June 17, 2018, to cancer at age 68, those of us who read her—depended on her for guidance and to madden and sometimes sadden us—know what it was like to walk into a cool and semi-darkened theater of any sort, look around for familiar faces or the usual theater donors and nerds, and spot Jackie: laser-focused, gaze fixed straight ahead as if to ignore even herself, and observe the wracked nerves her very presence in an auditorium could cause.

Her reporter's note pad was never fully visible but always certainly there, perhaps expertly balanced on a knee, her pen poised and slightly elevated like the conductor's baton it was. When the lights went down, so did the tip of her pen, like the stylus on a thrilling, new and difficult record album.

The sound? Her review in the next day's *Enquirer*.

The fury? The group exhalation of anyone (writer, director, actors, techs) who had a hand in the production witnessed—praised or eviscerated—by Jackie.

Actress Torie Wiggins says Jackie remained true to her mission and herself despite what the theater community thought of her and her reviews.

"Thank God, she liked me. For a food critic-turned-regional theater critic—it's important to note this because actors often brought this up to discredit her when she criticized their work on stage. She was brutally honest. It helped some and hurt others. She may not have told the truth, but she told a truth, one that was always published. She would sit right in (the actor's) sightline and make every effort to show absolutely no emotion, although a few times I caught her laughing. One thing is for sure: She loved theater. She really did."

Jackie is largely credited by producing directors with nurturing and furthering Cincinnati's nascent mid-1990s theater community.

Critics occupy that rare position among us. We know they're there, but we also know not to approach without permission—they are rare and exotic and temperamental birds, no doubt; however, there's a strange and unspoken rule at play. We all know the critic must reside among us mere seers who live without the gift of articulating and imparting opinion for general consumption.

But Jackie was blessed in two ways. In the first, her job was literally to see art, usually at night, sometimes on weekends, and often in off-beat locations. Secondly, what she thought of that art was read by and mattered to the citizens and art makers of this city (and beyond). And who knows if she carried the gravitas of all that around with her or if she abused it and participated in off-the-page pissing matches?

For 19-plus years, Jackie documented art of the ages, and in this way, she left documents of time and place. Jackie Demaline is an old-school throwback to a time when Cincinnatians consumed two daily newspapers, and when the writers therein held not only name-brand recognition but also the heft and seriousness that reputation carried with it.

But even in the absence of her physical being, her name and what it meant to us is still wholly recognizable.

—Kathy Y. Wilson

MARY EMERY

1844–1927

Look all around Cincinnati and you will see evidence of the life and bountiful good works of Mary Emery. More than 90 years after her passing, Emery's contributions are still very much alive.

Mary Emery was born Mary Muhlenberg Hopkins in Brooklyn, New York. Educated at the Packer Collegiate Institute at the age of 16, she studied mathematics and astronomy, subjects generally reserved for young men.

At age 18, she and her family moved to Cincinnati where she met and married Thomas J. Emery. Thomas was the eldest son of the Emery family who made their fortune in real estate and also by industrially converting the animal byproducts of "Porkopolis" to dripless candles, lamp oil, and chemicals.

Charity and generosity were central in their lives. Throughout their 40-year marriage, the Emerys actively sought to improve the circumstances of those in need no matter their economic status or ethnicity. They were instrumental in developing Cincinnati Children's Hospital, the Orphan Asylum for Colored Children, and the Fresh Air Farm and Society.

Yet her life was not without its own tragedy. At 16, her son Albert was killed in a sledding accident, and seven years later, son Sheldon died of an infection. In 1906, Thomas died while on a trip to the Middle East.

Mary turned grief into giving. She managed the $20 million family fortune with what she called a vast responsibility. Among her gifts was $100,000 to the Cincinnati Art Museum for the Thomas J. Emery Free Day Endowment. Through this gift, the public had—and still has—the opportunity to see great art with free general admission each Saturday.

Two of Emery's passions came together a century ago with the help of a good friend: she and Anna Sinton Taft rescued the failing Cincinnati Zoo in 1916, and both were major patrons to help form the Cincinnati Opera Association in 1920. Emery and Taft operated the Zoo until their deaths, at which point the city took it over. For more than 50 years, Cincinnati Summer Opera performed at the Zoo. Cincinnati's Zoo and Opera are second oldest in the country in their respective categories, after the Philadelphia Zoo and the Metropolitan Opera, respectively.

Emery was a prolific art collector. Traveling the world, she procured a significant collection of old masters valued at $3.5 million at her death in 1927. She bequeathed it to the Cincinnati Art Museum along with funds for a building to house it.

As a memorial to her late husband, Emery funded a new building for The Ohio Mechanics Institute (now the Ohio College of Applied Science), important in the development of Cincinnati's machine tool industry. It included Emery Hall, a state-of-the-art auditorium designed for public use. The acoustical quality was legendary. The Cincinnati Symphony Orchestra called it home from 1912–1936.

Perhaps her greatest gift to Cincinnati is the Village of Mariemont. Named for her summer home in Rhode Island, Mariemont is a planned community east of downtown Cincinnati. Appalled by living conditions in the city, Emery wanted to create a national example of a planned community that provided residents with high quality of life while still enjoying city advantages. Today nearly 3,500 people call Mariemont home.

Mary Emery was shy and reserved. She avoided public attention for her good works. But through them, she was bold, determined and generous, leaving her imprint on Cincinnati and a legacy for the ages.

—Susan Fellows Crabtree

Nota bene: See also Anna Sinton Taft Essay on page 27.

CAROL ANN HAILE

1924–2004

Carol Ann Haile. The name sounds familiar if you've spent time exploring Cincinnati, especially its riverfront, where the whimsical animals of Carol Ann's Carousel, a gift from the Carol Ann and Ralph V. Haile, Jr. / U.S. Bank Foundation, delights visitors of all ages.

The foundation, which supports a wide variety of cultural and community efforts across Greater Cincinnati, continues the work that Carol Ann championed throughout her 80 years.

Carol Ann Haile was born in 1924 to Viola Pebworth and Clifford Homan, president and CEO of Peoples Liberty Bank. Raised in Fort Mitchell, Carol Ann was an alumna of Miss Doherty's School. Now a part of Seven Hills School in Cincinnati, Miss Doherty's was founded by Mary Harlan Doherty, a woman who believed that women should be as prepared for college as they were for social endeavors. The school encouraged young women to strive for excellence, hard work, and service, advice Carol Ann appears to have followed throughout her life.

Years of volunteerism for the United Way, fine arts, health care, and senior service organizations began for Carol Ann during World War II when she was a driver for the Red Cross Motor Corps. She also became deeply involved with the Junior League of Cincinnati, and it was out of this work that Carol Ann became involved with the Cincinnati Art Museum. In 1960, Carol Ann helped the Junior League establish the museum's docent program, and she was one of the founders of the museum shop, which began in 1969. She served on the museum's Volunteer Advisory Council from its inception in 1975, and as one of the museum shop managers into the 1990s.

Her work at the Cincinnati Art Museum blended Carol Ann's love of art and architecture. "She loved all beautiful things," with her outgoing personality and practical know-how, said Tim Maloney, a close friend and president and CEO of the Haile Foundation. As the daughter of a bank president, Carol Ann graduated from Randolph Macon Women's College with a math degree. She was wicked smart and understood the importance of revenue.

In 1947, in a candlelight ceremony, Carol Ann married Ralph V. Haile, who would go on to run Peoples Liberty Bank after her father's death in 1969. The couple supported and coordinated philanthropic efforts in Cincinnati and Northern Kentucky throughout their marriage, giving millions of dollars over the years to cultural and educational institutions, including Music Hall and Northern Kentucky University, and advocating for public funding for iconic regional institutions such as the Cincinnati Museum Center. With endless enthusiasm and charm, Carol Ann organized countless parties and fundraising events, and, Maloney said, she was as happy in the kitchen as she was at the VIP table.

Maloney and those who served with her at Cincinnati Art Museum and other organizations remember Carol Ann for her quick wit and bright smile—always welcoming, always laughing, always ready to help make Cincinnati a little better, a little more beautiful.

—Hillary Copsey

CAROL ANN'S CAROUSEL IN FRONT OF THE JOHN A. ROEBLING SUSPENSION BRIDGE

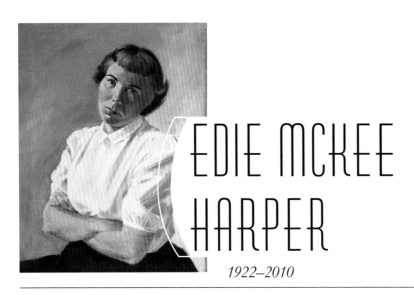

EDIE MCKEE HARPER

1922–2010

Edie Harper's vibrant cultural legacy lives on. Harper mastered and worked in multiple art media: drawing, painting, serigraphy, lithography, etching, enameling, photography, bead-making, sculpture and weaving.

Old and New Testament stories, childhood memories, and cats were her favorite subjects.

Edith Riley McKee was born in Kansas City, Missouri. She was a shy only child, the daughter of a restaurant owner and housewife, who had to devise her own amusements in small Missouri towns.

The McKees moved to Cincinnati in 1939 when young Edie's father accepted a job with Procter & Gamble. Harper graduated from Wyoming High School and entered the Art Academy of Cincinnati in 1940, already painting realistically at a level beyond her years. There Edie met fellow art student Charley Harper, who would become her husband.

In August 1947, Edie and Charley embarked on a six-month driving and painting honeymoon through America. They collaborated on their first silkscreens in 1948, a series of six nursery rhymes. During the 1950s, Harper painted canvasses with symbolic themes, explored her potential as a photographer at the frontiers of abstraction, and mixed the paints Charley used to print his vintage bird, travel and fish series.

The next decade was a gratifying period in Harper's career. During World War II, Harper had worked in a photography lab on war-related projects for the U.S. Corps of Engineers. Her proficiency in 8 x 10 photography later earned her a one-woman show of abstract images at the Contemporary Art Center of Cincinnati in 1961. Her serigraphs (silkscreen prints) were nationally represented by The Frame House Gallery of Louisville, Kentucky, from 1968 to 1990 and were popular with art collectors.

In the final decades of her life, Edie was given shows worthy of her stature at venues like the Weston Center for the Arts, the Contemporary Arts Center (for the second time), and the Cincinnati Art Museum. Her work has been reproduced on licensed stationery and books, posters and prints, houseware, puzzles, Rookwood ceramic tiles, and needle art pattern kits.

After her death in 2010, Harper's work gained even greater currency. In 2017, ArtWorks and its youth apprentices reworked her *Crazy Cat/Crazy Quilt* image as a wall mural, a modernist interpretation of her beloved calico cat, Katrinka. In 2019, The Carnegie held the Greater Cincinnati region's first retrospective exhibition of Harper's fluid work across media and styles, titled *E is for Edie*. Also in 2019, Harper's *Pigs Are Big* lithograph was chosen by *CityBeat* as its motif for Best of Cincinnati.

Harper was also a defender of animal welfare, domestic and wild. Her tender advocacy for creatures who cannot speak for themselves is one of the primary goals of the Edie and Charley Harper Foundation.

Edie's total body of artwork would be larger if she had been able to pursue her career full-time. However, she was also a homemaker and mother. Son Brett sums up her dilemma: "She sacrificed much of her creative life to raising me and establishing a warm, wonderful home for my father and me. I believe that someday the importance of her work will be internationally recognized."

—Kathy Merchant with Brett Harper

ELIZABETH "BETTY" WOHLGEMUTH HERSCHEDE

1912–1995

Elizabeth "Betty" Wohlgemuth Herschede was a significant patron of Cincinnati's arts. Her generous gifts, many of which were kept private, supported the Cincinnati Symphony Orchestra (CSO), the Cincinnati Ballet, Cincinnati Opera, and the Taft Museum of Art.

May Festival, WGUC public radio, and WCET public television were also beneficiaries. "My mother cared about the arts passionately, but she did not care about recognition," said Elizabeth D. Herschede. "She gave because she cared and loved those organizations. It never mattered to her if she was president of an organization or just licking stamps for it."

Born in 1912 to Edward J. Wohlgemuth and Stella Goss, Betty married John Zumstein Herschede in 1940. Their marriage represented a union between two prominent Cincinnati families, each having deep roots in the community. Mrs. Herschede's father had founded the National Underwriter Company in 1897, one of the first such companies to offer life insurance products. Her husband's grandfather, Frank (Franz) Herschede, had founded the family business originally known as the Herschede Hall Clock Company in 1877. Shortly after, the clock business expanded to include fine jewelry. The Zumstein family, for whom a street is named in Hyde Park, was also connected by marriage to the couple: John's maternal great-grandfather, also named John, was Cincinnati's Postmaster, and his maternal grandfather (Frank) was a Cincinnati publisher.

Rather than follow his father and brother Mark into the family business, John joined his wife's family's life insurance business, eventually becoming its president. Together, Betty and John had three daughters.

Herschede was an active supporter of the CSO beginning in the early 1950s. In the "For Women" column in the *Cincinnati Enquirer*, it stated that "Mrs. Herschede had one of her happiest symphony experiences as chairman of 'Young People' in

1955—the 60th season anniversary." In 1961, as head of the Cincinnati Symphony Women's Committee, she was inspired by a program in Cleveland to create "Musical Panoramas," a popular music-literary series consisting of 10 study sessions on the topics of symphony and composers. The subject matter was later expanded to include opera and related themes from literature, art, and ballet, and was open to the public. Herschede also served at various times as a CSO trustee, and a member of the board of overseers.

Herschede was a life long member of the Taft Museum of Art, a life trustee of the Cincinnati Institute of Fine Arts, and a life trustee of the Cincinnati Opera. She was also an honorary board member of the Cincinnati Ballet.

The private Wohlgemuth Herschede Foundation was established a year before Mrs. Herschede's death. Now in its 25th year of operation, c/o Fifth Third Bank, the Foundation has over $12 million in assets and annually distributes over a half million dollars in small grants to local nonprofit organizations.

In her August 11, 1995, obituary, Wayne Godwin, former president of WCET, said Mrs. Herschede's legacy "is one of unparalleled philanthropy to our community, borne of her unbridled faith in and love for its people. Her outstanding support for Channel 48 and public television was a testament to her unselfish willingness to share with the entire community."

Upon her passing, WGUC dedicated an entire day of its programming to her memory.

—Ilene Ross Tucker

MARY ELLYN HUTTON
1940–2018

Mary Ellyn will be remembered as a journalist with unflagging dedication to Cincinnati's musical arts. The classical music critic for the *Cincinnati Post* covered the classical scene for more than a decade after the demise of Cincinnati's afternoon newspaper in 2007.

She was named Best Critic in Ohio for print publications under 100,000 by the Ohio Society of Professional Journalists in 2008.

A classically trained musician, Hutton was a meticulous writer who chronicled and critiqued all of Cincinnati's classical music institutions, large and small. She went on tours with the Cincinnati Symphony Orchestra, and in the days before widespread Internet, took along her own typewriter so that she could fax her reports back from hotels abroad.

"Mary Ellyn was a delight to work with and infinitely increased the classiness quotient of the *Post*," said Keith Herrell, who worked at the afternoon daily for 24 years, including as features editor from 1996–2001. "She wasn't just a critic—she could wear a reporter's hat, too, and wear it well. The community was enriched by her knowledge."

Hutton wrote for 23 years for the *Post*, starting in 1984. On January 1, 2008, the day after it closed its doors, she wrote on her website, "I will remember the knot in my gut writing on deadline Friday nights, the twinge every time I checked the paper the next day and the constant, uphill battle of making the *Post* matter to the social register mentality of Cincinnati's arts community."

Arts journalism wasn't a job. It was her mission, said Tom Consolo, a former *Post* copy editor through its last decade. "I teased Mary Ellyn sometimes that she never heard a concert she didn't like," he said. "Partly because of her own training as a performer, music was such a source of joy to her."

After the daily closed, Mrs. Hutton established *musicincincinnati.com*, which was named Best Web Site by the Greater Cincinnati Chapter of the Society of Professional Journalists. Cincinnati Opera artistic director Evans Mirageas said about the new digital format, "I relished Mary Ellyn's blog posts, especially since space considerations no longer constrained her elegant prose."

In addition to her work for the *Cincinnati Post*, Hutton wrote articles and reviews for the *Cincinnati Enquirer*, *Detroit Free Press*, *Newark Star Ledger*, *San Antonio Light*, Musical America (*musicalamerica.com*), *Opera News* and many other news outlets and music publications.

Born in Lexington, Kentucky, Hutton was trained as a violist, graduating from the University of Kentucky. She earned a master's degree in music history from Yale University and a law degree from the University of Kentucky College of Law. She practiced law in Kentucky and Texas before returning to her first love, music.

She was principal violist of the University of Kentucky Symphony Orchestra and played viola in the New Haven Symphony Orchestra while at Yale. She served as associate principal violist of the Lexington (Kentucky) Philharmonic Orchestra from 1971–80).

She married Dr. John J. Hutton in Lexington. The couple moved to Cincinnati in 1984, and her husband served as the longtime dean of the University of Cincinnati College of Medicine and director of the Biomedical Informatics Division at Cincinnati Children's Hospital Medical Center. Dr. Hutton pre-deceased his wife in 2016.

—Janelle Gelfand

IRMA LAZARUS
1913–1993

"Where she was, the action was, the party was, the fun was." If there is anyone who could be called "Cincinnati's First Lady of the Arts," it is Irma Lazarus. For 50 years, she dedicated her life to the advancement of the arts.

Born in Brooklyn in 1913 and a graduate of Smith College in 1934, Lazarus founded the Ohio Arts Council in 1965, served as its chairperson from 1973–1975, and was noted for her frequent travels to rural Ohio to garner support for the Council.

Bluegrass pioneer Katie Laur recalls Lazarus traveling with her good friend, Jim Edgy (another leader of the development of the arts in Ohio), in his vintage Volkswagon convertible to small towns to promote the arts. Laur recalls how Lazarus would bring her thermos of coffee and hard-boiled eggs to enjoy along the way. One can imagine her hair softly blowing in the breeze as the two planned their solicitations of support to grow the arts.

Lazarus' legacy of growing people's interest in the arts began in the 1960s. Along with Phyllis Weston, Lazarus founded Young Friends of the Arts. This new organization sought to introduce students at the University of Cincinnati's College Conservatory of Music to the Cincinnati Symphony Orchestra (CSO), and to encourage other young people to attend and enjoy the arts. Just a few dollars were required to join the pioneering group (which became Enjoy the Arts in 1981 and has since merged with ArtsWave). Lazarus also served on the boards of the Cincinnati Symphony, Ballet, and Opera, as well as the American Symphony Orchestra. In her later years, she became an active fundraiser for AIDS-relief volunteers of Cincinnati.

Lazarus was also a forerunner in television. WCET (Channel 48) was one of the country's first public television stations, and it introduced a new game show called *Culture Anyone?* in 1966. The host? Of course, it was Irma. The show was later named *Conversations with Irma*. The show focused on the arts and was one of the most popular shows on Channel 48.

Lazarus enjoyed life fully, and her athletic skills undoubtedly gave her the enormous energy to lead the local arts community. When she was not advocating for the arts, she often rode one of her horses to hunt in Indian Hill and surrounding areas as a member of the Camargo Hunt Club. She was an avid skier who loved the slopes in Vail, Colorado, and an avid tennis player on her home court, who disdained the occasional injury. After breaking her coccyx, only a few hours later she was off to another meeting of the CSO!

She also loved dancing with her husband Fred and hosting parties at their home. Her friends included countless celebrities, politicians, musicians (she had a particular love for music), and arts patrons. The socialite's turquoise swimming pool was a welcoming sight for her frequent guests, who enjoyed the Lazarus' private retreat surrounded by bougainvillea plants, wildflowers, and great trees that provided privacy.

In 1987, Enjoy the Arts celebrated her achievements with a black-tie event that included some of her out-of-town friends to perform or speak. Her favorite celebrity friend, Leonard Bernstein, stole the show with a poem he had composed. Top to bottom, the first letter of each line spelled IRMA LAZARUS.

Indeed, the first name that should pop out in any discussion about arts in Cincinnati is IRMA LAZARUS.
—Randy Freking

RUTH LYONS

1905–1988

Every weekday at noon, folks all across Cincinnati invited Ruth Lyons into their homes as host of *The 50-50 Club* on WLWT-TV. The most popular daytime television show in the nation had seven million viewers, even though it was a regional show.

With her blonde coiffure, a string of pearls, white gloves, and a microphone hidden in a bouquet, the First Lady of Television set the standards for what people talked about, what products they bought, even how they celebrated Christmas. Her live, un-scripted show with music and whatever guests were visiting Cincinnati at the time, from Liberace to Bob Hope, was the foundation of the talk show format. "Ruth Lyons was the Oprah Winfrey of her day, a day-time Jack Paar," film star Angie Dickinson once said.

The broadcasting pioneer stumbled into the business. In May 1929, while working as a pianist for WKRC radio, Lyons was asked to fill in one day as the host of *A Woman's Hour*. She found the script too boring, so she began chatting about whatever came to mind. "The script was forgotten, and I felt as though I was talking to people out there in radio land, who were interested in as many things as I was," Lyons recalled.

She was heralded for her role as the soothing voice on the radio during the severe flood in 1937, remaining on the air for several days to provide listeners with information.

Lyons switched over to Powel Crosley, Jr.'s WSAI and WLW stations in 1942, hosting *Petticoat Party-line*, an afternoon show for women, and *Morning Matinee*. An audience of 50 women was invited to attend the live radio broadcast for a new show in 1946 that Lyons called *The 50 Club*, which became

her signature show. When the audience doubled in the Crosley Square studio, the show moved to tele-vision in 1949 as *The 50/50 Club*, creating a whole new learning experience for Lyons in front of the camera, but that is where she really innovated.

Her influence went beyond ratings. In 1939, during a performance at Cincinnati Children's Hospi-tal, Lyons found the hospital depressing and so asked her listeners to pitch in for toys for the children that Christmas. Lyons went down to Arnold's Fairyland toyshop and bought gifts, then held a Christmas party at the hospital. Since then, the Ruth Lyons Children's Fund has given more than $20 million to children in Cincinnati-area hospitals.

There was no doubt that Lyons was in charge, with the last word on production and even sponsors. She refused to promote any product she didn't like personally. Biographer Michael A. Banks noted, "She laid the foundation for women in television, not just as a talk show host, but also for women executives."

After suffering from health issues and the death of her adopted daughter, Candy Newman, of cancer, Lyons put down her microphone in January 1967. "Underneath it all, she was a regular person," said Banks. "That got her the big fan base. So many people said, 'Watching Ruth Lyons is like having a friend over for coffee.' "

—Jeff Suess

LORETTA MANGGRUM

1896–1992

It seems that music was pumping through Dr. Loretta C. Manggrum's veins from an early age. Following in the footsteps of her mother, who played the guitar and piano, Manggrum began playing the piano at church when she was six years old.

By the time she was a teenager, she was earning a weekly wage playing with a small orchestra in Huntington, West Virginia. But any dreams she may have had were put on hold when she dropped out of high school to take care of her mother when she became ill. Even then, music was never far from her mind.

While she, her husband and children lived in Pittsburgh, Manggrum supplemented the family's income by playing the piano during silent films at the local movie house. After moving to Cincinnati, where she raised several children and tended to the household while her husband ran a pharmacy, she went back to finish high school, graduating at the age of 49 in 1945. She then went on to earn a bachelor's degree in music from The Ohio State University (1951) and a master's degree from the Cincinnati Conservatory of Music (the precursor to University of Cincinnati's College-Conservatory of Music) in 1953. She was the first African American to graduate from the school.

It was during this time of breaking through boundaries that she composed and published what would come to be known as the Loretta Manggrum Collection: seven cantatas (vocal compositions with an instrumental accompaniment) written and performed by her church's choir during the 1940s and '50s, including *Christ Our Lord* (1953) and *Watch* (1958). Now part of the U.S. Library of Congress, the cantatas and other original works are supplemented by handwritten notes with personal comments from Manggrum herself.

Manggrum's legacy lives on today through the Loretta C. Manggrum Chorale. Comprised of volunteer members from Cincinnati churches, the group performs sacred music to provide scholarships for piano and organ students at the College-Conservatory of Music (CCM). The director of the organization is Eric V. Oliver, a former student and mentee of the musician, who organized the first concert of Manggrum's music in her honor in 2010.

"Mrs. Manggrum was just a masterful composer," said Oliver, who heads the Ministry of Music at Cincinnati's Zion Baptist Church. "The way she moves from key to key so smoothly is just brilliant. Some of her cantatas are extremely difficult and can be compared to Beethoven and Bach."

After her husband died in 1955, Manggrum set her sights on a new teaching career. She spent a decade teaching music at Garfield School before returning to CCM at the age of 80 to pursue a doctorate degree. In 1985, the school awarded her an honorary doctorate in music theory and composition.

"I think of her as being a local icon, and I don't think that she has gotten the attention she deserves," Oliver noted. "She came along at a time when blacks and females were not getting much attention (in classical music)."

—Aiesha D. Little

MARY LOUISE McLAUGHLIN
1847–1939

Mary (M.) Louise McLaughlin made an indelible global impact as one of the most celebrated ceramic artists in the world, though in her early career days she was often overshadowed by those around her.

Her brother, James W. McLaughlin, was a prominent Cincinnati architect who designed some of the city's most celebrated buildings, including the Old Main Library and the Cincinnati Art Museum. As for accomplishments with ceramics, she stood side by side with her more famous rival, Rookwood Pottery founder, Maria Longworth Nichols Storer.

Two leading ceramics artists who would make Cincinnati the cradle of American art pottery began by taking china painting classes from Benn Pitman and others at the McMicken School of Design (now the Art Academy of Cincinnati). Their art instruction was part of encouraging industrial arts with the decorative arts. McLaughlin graduated in 1877 and later that year published *China Painting: A Practical Manual for the Use of Amateurs in the Decoration of Hard Porcelain*, an influential book aimed at women that sold 20,000 copies and helped launch the china painting movement.

On April 1, 1879, McLaughlin formed the Cincinnati Pottery Club "to promote the growth of ceramic art in Cincinnati" and served as the first president, with accomplished china painter, Clara Chipman Newton, as secretary. The invitation sent to Maria Longworth Nichols—then married to first husband George Nichols, who died in 1885—was apparently lost. Nichols took the slight as an affront and refused to join the Pottery Club.

Sometime around 1878 (there is some discrepancy in dates), McLaughlin discovered a technique for decorating pottery under the glaze. She was celebrated for her *Ali Baba* vase, made in 1880, as the largest pottery ever made using the underglaze technique. Not to be outdone, Nichols made her own elaborate vase—*Aladdin*—using underglaze decoration. That same year, Nichols founded the Rookwood Pottery Co., funded by her family's fortune. Rookwood, which employed McLaughlin's underglaze slip technique, became renowned across the globe, with the recognition bestowed on Nichols (who remarried in 1886 and is best known today as Maria Longworth Storer).

The rivalry was reignited when Rookwood used McLaughlin's technique and attempted to refute McLaughlin's claims of discovering the method. The method had in fact been patented by a third party, Mr. T. J. Wheatley, who never tried to defend it. McLaughlin wrote to Nichols claiming that Rookwood was "indebted to me for the original idea and that my process is the foundation principle of that now in use there.… Any true history of the introduction of this pottery into Cincinnati must give me credit for having furnished the idea upon which the industry has been founded."

Initially stung by the loss of recognition for her contribution to Cincinnati's history of decorative pottery, she was vindicated in 1938 when the American Ceramic Society officially recognized McLaughlin for discovering the principles for the underglaze technique used by Rookwood.

—Jeff Suess

LOUISE NIPPERT

1911–2012

Louise Dieterle Nippert's generosity is evident throughout the city she loved. The *Cincinnati Enquirer* described her as "the last of an extraordinary generation of patrons who loved the arts passionately and gave generously to keep them alive."

Nippert was a fourth generation Cincinnatian born August 27, 1911. A life-long lover of music, she earned her Bachelor of Arts degree from the University of Cincinnati in 1934 and was a mezzo soprano professionally trained through the Cincinnati College-Conservatory of Music (CCM). She married attorney and Gamble family heir Louis Nippert at the Mount Auburn Presbyterian Church on June 1, 1935.

Louise and Louis were a powerful philanthropic couple, donating hundreds of millions of dollars to the arts, education, sports, and preservation. Childless, they preferred to work quietly and often anonymously, filling needs in the city to help ensure a vibrant community.

And what was more vibrant than the Cincinnati Reds baseball team? In 1966, the team threatened to leave the Queen City. The Nipperts joined an investment group and purchased the club. They were majority owners from 1973–1981 (which included World Series Championship years 1975 and 1976). Nippert kept a minority position in the Club until her death, making the Nipperts' 46-year ownership the longest in franchise history. "No person loved the Cincinnati Reds more than Mrs. Nippert, and her players loved her for her devotion to the family atmosphere she fostered within the organization," said current Reds president Bob Castellini.

While she loved the Reds, her true passion was music and the arts. After her husband's death in 1992, she funded the University of Cincinnati's renovation of the Dieterle Vocal Arts Center, honoring her parents. It houses CCM's voice, opera, choral, and accompanying departments. In addition, Nippert endowed a number of scholarships and chairs including the first endowed chair for CCM.

Her most enduring legacy comes through the Greenacres Foundation established by the Nipperts in 1988. They transformed their Indian Hill estate and gardens into an educational and cultural center to preserve the woodlands and farmlands for future generations. In 2009, Nippert infused the foundation with $185 million, designating $100 million to endow its programs. This donation made her the fifth largest charitable contributor in the country that year, according to *Slate 60: Donor Bios*. Today, the Greenacres Foundation serves more than 30,000 students a year, encouraging conservation, music, and culture.

Importantly, she earmarked $85 million to establish the Louise Dieterle Nippert Musical Arts Fund to support classical music in Cincinnati. Over the years she gave generously to Cincinnati's Music Hall and the Cincinnati Symphony Orchestra (CSO). At 98, she ensured her passion could be sustained for generations, and the CSO was the primary beneficiary. She gave this nearly 125-year-old cultural hub the means to remain a dynamic part of the city's fabric. The Cincinnati Opera and Cincinnati Ballet benefitted, too. Her gift has enabled them to engage the CSO for performances and keep Music Hall as their home theater.

The history, life and legacy of Louise Dieterle Nippert are deeply rooted in Cincinnati. The crack of a baseball hitting a bat, the crescendo in a classical symphony, and a lilting birdsong—all of these are reminders of the indelible mark she left on the city.

—Susan Fellows Crabtree

ELIZABETH NOURSE

1859–1938

When Elizabeth Nourse stepped out into the art world as a Salon painter in the late 1880s, not many women had made art their career. Female students were expected to teach or to follow their art as a hobby after they were married. Nourse had other ideas.

Elizabeth and her twin sister, Adelaide, were born October 26, 1859, in Mount Healthy in Cincinnati, the youngest of ten children. At age fourteen, the twins attended McMicken School of Design, then part of the University of Cincinnati (and later the Art Academy of Cincinnati). While Adelaide preferred the woodcarving courses and went on to marry the instructor, Benn Pitman, Elizabeth studied it all—drawing, painting, carving, sculpture. She was one of the first to take advantage of life classes offered to female students at the school. Nourse completed her courses in 1881 and was offered a position teaching drawing, but she declined so she could focus on painting.

In 1887, accompanied by her older sister Louise, Nourse went to Paris to study at the Académie Julian. After three months, she was told she needed no more instruction, but the art world was not so open to women artists. She had to prove to the male jurists that she was a serious artist. Nourse submitted her painting *La mère (The Mother)* to the Société des Artistes Français, known simply as the Salon. The jury hung the piece on line with eye-level, a rather prominent position for an unknown artist.

Nourse was a Realist painter, often depicting peasant women and working women in an unideal-ized manner. When it was suggested that she could paint more attractive subjects that would be easier to sell, she replied, "How can I paint what does not appeal to me?" Cincinnati sculptor Clement Barnhorn called Nourse "unquestionably the premier woman artiste of America." She was only the second woman to be selected as a member of the Société Nationale des Beaux Arts, or the New Salon.

When World War I erupted in 1914, the Nourse sisters remained in their adopted land to help with the sick and wounded. Nourse underwent surgery for breast cancer in 1920 and did little painting after that. Modern art styles altered tastes, and Nourse's Realism fell out of favor. After her death on October 8, 1938, her work was largely forgotten until the 1980s when Cincinnati native Mary Alice Heekin Burke wrote her art history master's thesis on Nourse and rekindled interest in the artist's work.

Today, Nourse's paintings are part of the Cincinnati Art Museum's Cincinnati Wing, her sketchbooks are displayed at the Mercantile Library, and her *Self-Portrait* was recreated for an ArtWorks mural at Eighth and Walnut streets in downtown Cincinnati.

—Jeff Suess

HARRIET MARSH PAGE

1932–2013

Remembered for being a fierce and dedicated advocate and promoter of black classical artists, Harriet Marsh Page was one of the first black women to serve on the Cincinnati Opera's board of trustees. She helped make inclusion a priority for the organization.

Director and CEO Patricia K. Beggs said that Marsh Page profoundly influenced her and helped shape her approach to diversity and inclusion from the very beginning of her time at the Opera, making diversity in casting a top priority when they hired new artistic directors in 1996 and 2005.

"Our company led the way in our industry in recognizing and taking intentional and thoughtful steps toward making the Opera, Music Hall, and the arts in general more welcoming and inclusive of all people," Beggs noted. "Harriett and others played a huge role in those early days. Because of this group's efforts, we made diversity a company mandate in soliciting board members and hiring staff, seasonal employees, and artists."

It wasn't just the opera community that felt Marsh Page's influence. Through her music program *The Marsh Series*, she engaged, hosted, mentored and showcased some of the most talented up-and-com-

ing and world-renowned black singers and musicians. The series was the country's oldest recital of African American performers and composers. In addition to recitals, the series sponsored workshops, master classes, and lectures/demonstrations at area schools and for local community groups.

Norman Johns, a cellist for the Cincinnati Symphony Orchestra, and Jim Jones, former historian for the Cincinnati chapter of the National Association for the Advancement of Colored People, coordinated a memorial service for Marsh Page after her death.

"Harriet was a person who motivated the community to get interested in the orchestra in a much more impactful way," said Johns, who performed as part of *The Marsh Series* in the late 1970s. "Harriet got the ball rolling and piqued the interests of the arts community and churches. She tried to do a lot of progressive things in the arts."

—Aiesha D. Little

NORMA PETERSEN

1928–2016

Norma Petersen got things done. A veteran volunteer for many of Cincinnati's outstanding musical organizations, her personal commitment to volunteering made her the perfect choice to organize and lead other volunteers.

Petersen and her husband Gerry grew up in Brigham City, Utah, and married in 1948. His position with Procter & Gamble brought them to Cincinnati in 1962. She immediately became involved with the Cincinnati Symphony Orchestra's Women's Committee, leading immensely successful subscription drives. In 1974, with Petersen as the ticket chair, sales jumped by more than fifty percent, from 11,000 to 17,000. She served as the Women's Committee's president from 1977 to 1979, coinciding with Erich Kunzel's appointment as music director of the Cincinnati Pops. He appreciated her devotion. The CSO hired her as its director of volunteers, a position she held for six years. She, said Kunzel, "knew the value of volunteers and was very supportive."

In 1987, she left the CSO to become executive director of the Cincinnati Chamber Orchestra, until 1995. During her tenure, Keith Lockhart was hired as its music director, the position he held before he was appointed music director of the Boston Pops.

Two years later, Kunzel asked her to help establish the Greater Cincinnati Arts and Education Center. He was the public champion. Petersen never sought the limelight while serving as its volunteer executive director. She was an indispensable organizer who kept the endeavor moving forward. Their efforts culminated in 2010 when the new School for Creative and Performing Arts opened two blocks from Cincinnati Music Hall.

An *Enquirer* Woman of the Year in 2000, Petersen served on numerous boards including the Cincinnati Ballet. She was a founding member and leader of the Over-the-Rhine Chamber of Commerce and the Society for the Preservation of Music Hall. For the latter, she played a key role in the installation of the Albee Wurlitzer Organ in Music Hall's Ballroom. She championed bringing the World Choir Games to Cincinnati in 2012.

Despite her extensive civic engagement, Petersen was also a devoted mother to six children who all graduated from Walnut Hills High School. Gerry died unexpectedly in 1994, but Norma never missed a beat in her devotion as a volunteer to Cincinnati's arts community.

Nominating Petersen in 2001 for the *Enquirer* Woman of the Year, fellow volunteer board member Marcella Hsiung called her "the archetype of the tireless community volunteer."

"I'm an optimist," Petersen once said. "It's about the future, it's about art, and it's all about kids fulfilling their lives. How can anyone get down when they're working for that?" Her life philosophy was "Just keep going. If there is a need for my service, I do it." And she did it well, ensuring a future for the arts and for young people in Cincinnati.

—Rick Pender

PATRICIA RENICK

1932–2007

"I was determined not to be among those rocking chair people on the front porch of the future, saddened by what might have been," sculptor Patricia Renick once explained to the Cincinnati Contemporary Arts Center (CAC).

"So I made a *Triceracopter*. It's as simple and as complex as that."

The *Triceracopter*, created in response to the Vietnam War, was the center of an exhibition of Renick's work by the CAC in late 1977. *Triceracopter* was a massive fiberglass installation, half dinosaur, half machine. In a catalog from the CAC exhibition, Laura H. Chapman described *Triceracopter* and its "improbable merging of animal, mechanical and human form" as an example of the larger themes that Renick explored in her art: "the mutations of spirit and identity that seem to characterize our time, the impact of technology on our sensibilities, and the varieties of obsolescence we can experience."

In 2003, Renick told the magazine *Sculpture*, "I did not see (*Triceracopter*) as a celebration, but as a cautionary tale, an expression of hope for the end of war. War is a dichotomy. It seduces the dream-self through heroic fantasy while threatening the physical self with extinction." Renick created *Triceracopter* from the shell of a U.S. Army OH-6A Cayuse combat helicopter. Today this sculpture of hope can be found at the University of Cincinnati's Langsam Library. (NKU's Steely Library is home to *Triceracopter*'s sibling, the similarly out sized *Stegowagenvolkssaurus*, a statement opposing the over dependence on fossil fuels.)

Though Renick grew up in Florida, she launched her career as a professional artist in Ohio after studying art education, printmaking and sculpture at The Ohio State University. In 1969, she began teaching at the University of Cincinnati's College of Design, Architecture, Art, and Planning, a tenure which would last over 30 years. In the early 1970s, Renick's work was featured at the Cincinnati Art Museum, the CAC, the Taft Museum of Art, Closson's Gallery, and more.

"Mother Art," as Renick would be nicknamed, received the prestigious Corbett Award in 1975, honoring her outstanding contributions by an individual artist to the cultural vitality of Cincinnati. Of the "National Sculpture Conference: Works by Women" that she mounted in Cincinnati 1987, Renick told *Sculpture* that she "thought the time was right for women sculptors to come together and overcome their sense of isolation." A staggering number of 1,200 people were in attendance.

Renick passed away in May of 2007, after which *CityBeat* described a parade of the artist's many friends and admirers gathering in front of Memorial Hall, each donning an outrageous hat "honoring the memory of sculptor, teacher, and notable hat-wearer Patricia Renick."

—Erica Reid

MAMIE SMITH

1883–1946

It ended up being fitting that singer Mamie Smith was billed as The Queen of the Blues in her heyday. In 2018, after years of speculation among blues historians and the music community, it was finally confirmed that she was from the Queen City of Cincinnati.

"The discovery of Mamie Smith's birthplace is a major event in music history and black history, but it is also a major event in Cincinnati history," said 2018 Guggenheim Fellow John Jeremiah Sullivan, who traced Smith's lineage to downtown Cincinnati through a variety of historical records. "Any place that [she] was born has a claim on being a Birthplace of the Blues. You're talking about the whole history of commercial American pop music in the twentieth century, rock 'n' roll, everything. Mamie stands at the beginning of that."

And what a beginning it was. In 1920, Smith recorded "That Thing Called Love"/"You Can't Keep a Good Man Down" for OKeh Records, which is said to be the first blues recording ever sung by an African-American woman. That same year, the record label released her version of "Crazy Blues" which eventually sold one million copies, making the Cincinnati native a bona fide star. The song's success was at the epicenter of the rise of what was known as race records, early 20th century music made exclusively by and for African Americans. The music crossed over and began to attract white audiences, playing a pivotal role in what would become the *de facto* desegregation of the American recording industry.

A few days before her performance in front of a sold-out crowd at Richmond, Indiana's 2,500-seat venue Richmond Coliseum, the *Richmond Palladium*

and *Sun-Telegram* claimed that Smith "has done more than any other singer perhaps in America to popularize the genuine 'blues' song of the day" and called her song delivery the ability to create "living, potent things charged with a pulsing and individual rhythm."

Smith was a quadruple threat—she sang, danced, acted, and played the piano. While her contract with OKeh ended only a few years after she recorded "Crazy Love," she spent most of the 1920s touring with her Jazz Hounds and appearing in movies and shorts, including *Jailhouse Blues* (1929), *Paradise in Harlem* (1939), *Sunday Sinners* (1940), *Stolen Paradise* (1941), *Murder on Lenox Avenue* (1941) and *Because I Love You* (1941).

Smith was laid to rest at Frederick Douglass Memorial Park in Staten Island, New York, in 1946. In 2014, through several fundraisers and crowdfunding campaigns, blues and other music enthusiasts raised enough to erect a granite monument at her gravesite. The monument was unveiled September 2014 at a music-filled memorial and dedication, shortly before the 68th anniversary of her death.

"Crazy Blues" was officially inducted into the Grammy Hall of Fame in 1994. In 2005, the song was selected for permanent preservation in the National Recording Registry at the Library of Congress.

—Aiesha D. Little

HARRIET BEECHER STOWE

1811–1896

The most unfortunate part of Harriet Beecher Stowe's name being synonymous with her contentious antislavery novel, *Uncle Tom's Cabin*, is that it overshadows her development as an author and abolitionist.

It also draws attention away from *Dred*, her second and more informed work about slavery.

In the 40 years leading up to her most renowned book being published, Stowe developed her love of writing at a school for young women founded by her oldest sister, Catharine, in her birthplace of Connecticut. When Stowe's father, Dr. Lyman Beecher, became president of Lane Theological Seminary in Cincinnati, she moved there with her family at age 21.

Cincinnati birthed her formative years as a woman and a writer. She joined a literary group called the Semi-Colon Club. Stowe's first story was published shortly thereafter. The Semi-Colon Club is also where Stowe met Calvin Stowe—the man who would eventually become her husband—and Eliza Stowe, Calvin's first wife who became Harriet's close friend before dying from cholera.

Stowe's proximity to the slave state of Kentucky prompted brushes with fugitive slaves, former slaves, and fellow abolitionists. These encounters would inspire her writing of *Uncle Tom's Cabin*, which began as a series in the abolitionist paper *The National Era*. Using 21st century terminology, we could say that Stowe used her white-woman privilege to communicate slavery's atrocities to other privileged white people. But Stowe said the novel came to her in visions from God.

Uncle Tom's Cabin was a blessing to Stowe. It gave her an international platform to denounce slavery in front of European audiences and allowed her to provide well for her family. But generationally, particularly among descendants of black American slaves, the book is often viewed as a curse that perpetuates hackneyed stereotypes.

Black historians, writers, and cultural critics still wrestle with her depiction of the passive slave protagonist, Uncle Tom. African Americans use the derogatory term "Uncle Tom" for blacks who comply with white supremacy. More than 100 years after *Uncle Tom's Cabin* was published, Langston Hughes called it "the most cussed and discussed book of its time." James Baldwin said it was a "very bad novel" and compared its sentimentality with that of Louisa May Alcott's *Little Women*.

During the four years between *Uncle Tom's Cabin* (1852) and *Dred* (1856), Stowe developed a rapport with African-American abolitionists Sojourner Truth and Frederick Douglass. Douglass, whose autobiography was published seven years before *Uncle Tom's Cabin*, was one of Stowe's early critics. We can surmise that hearing Truth's and Douglass's stories of slavery and freedom influenced Stowe's perspective as she prepared to write the more revolutionist-leaning *Dred*.

It was during this period that Stowe completely disavowed her father's colonizationist philosophy and became an outright abolitionist. Later in life, she used her fortunes to start an integrated school for children and adults in Florida.

Cincinnati's tribute to Harriet Beecher Stowe is the house where she once lived in Walnut Hills, on Gilbert Avenue. From 1939 through the 1940s, the house was called "The Edgemont Inn" in the *Green Motorist Book*. It was one of few taverns listed in the travel guide as safe for African Americans in Cincinnati.

In 1949, the HBS House was opened to the public, and has remained a living history museum ever since. Hartford, Connecticut, claims her as well: the Harriet Beecher Stowe Center is a historical place museum preserving her Connecticut home, artifacts, and historical collections.

—Devin Parrish

ARALEE STRANGE

1943–2013

Aralee Strange was a poet. She was a poet's poet. And she was an artist's poet, too. While she offered inspiration to fellow writers, her poems inspired and garnered respect from many visual artists.

She saw a symbiotic relationship between the two art forms and fostered it through her projects. Her work has been called by her admirers "chiropractics for the soul."

Born in Birmingham, Alabama, December 5, 1943, Strange spent her working life in Atlanta, Georgia; Cambridge, Massachusetts; and New York City. She finally settled in Cincinnati where she lived for more than 20 years. A consummate artist, Strange was described by a friend as a "Jane-of-all-artistic-trades: a poet, filmmaker and performer."

Living in Cincinnati in the 1990s, she lived among fellow artists on Main Street, and she may have been seen a time or two in the Main City Bar. Her sometimes rough surroundings informed her work. Unassuming, a bohemian, maybe, her gravelly Southern voice and the lightning bolt tattoo on her cheek emitted the image of a creative woman free in spirit. A passionate writer, she railed against injustice and revered beauty and love in the human condition. Her life was also about making connections: fellow writers needing inspiration, poets needing a platform to share their words, artists needing a palette from which to paint.

Posters promoting her projects were often created by artists moved by her poetry. *Etta Stone: A Film for Radio* (1990), which aired nationally on NPR stations, is one example. The woodcut poster by Jay Bolotin was inspired by a poem in the program, "prayer (a poem in a painting)."

Her play *dr. pain on main* (1991) was based on a series of poems commissioned and produced by Cincinnati Playhouse in the Park. Artist and friend Jim

Wainscott's painting of Strange was paired with her poem from the series *pain eclipsed* published in 1995 by Clay Street Press.

She also was interested in a poem-drawing project. A collaboration with Cincinnati Art Academy alumna, Michelle Red Elk, produced a drawing called "dog snake raven" to accompany Strange's poem "Blood of My Pen."

Highlights of her work also include *The Chronicles of Plague* (1992), a play commissioned and produced by Ensemble Theatre Cincinnati; *An Evening at the Sad Cafe* (1995) performed at the Ensemble Theatre Cincinnati and the Carnegie Arts Center in Covington, Kentucky; and *This Train* (1996-2001), a film starring Soupy Sales that she wrote, directed and edited.

She moved to Athens, Georgia, in 2007 and established the Athens Word of Mouth reading room to meet other poets. She led it until her death on June 15, 2013. Cincinnati poets Mark Flanigan and Jim Palmarini replicated the idea in Cincinnati. Both reading rooms are still keeping Strange's legacy alive, giving new poets and writers connections and a voice.

Excerpt from "Spelling It Out":

*you enter through the start of something intuitive
it's what stirs under every starry-eyed experience
lights with a breath you can't help
the emerging narrative*

*step into the center
shall we dance?*

—Susan Fellows Crabtree

ANNA SINTON TAFT

1852–1931

In her *New York Times* obituary, Anna Sinton Taft was identified as "Mrs. Charles Taft, publisher's widow and sister-in-law of the late president," William Howard Taft, but she had accomplished much on her own during her lifetime.

The only child of David Sinton, pioneer iron indus-trialist, she became the richest woman in Ohio upon his death in 1900. She lived her entire adult life in the 1820 Federal-style mansion on Pike Street purchased by her father in 1869 from Nicholas Longworth.

Anna Sinton Taft was distinguished not just by her wealth but by what she did with it, promoting music, fine arts and other philanthropic enterprises. She and her husband were among the original founders of the Cincinnati Art Museum. She was one of the founders of the Cincinnati Symphony Orchestra in 1895 and en-dowed it with $1 million. In 1916, she and Mary Emery bought the Cincinnati Zoo, the oldest in the country, to rescue it from financial failure. Under her patronage, operatic concerts were presented there weekly during the summer. In 1920, also with her friend Mary Emery, she founded the Cincinnati Opera, which continued to perform at the Zoo until 1972.

The Tafts had an enormous impact on the Lytle Park neighborhood, and Mrs. Taft was actively in-volved in building projects there. The Tafts covered half the cost of the Anna Louise Inn, which opened in 1909 on the south side of the park. Named for their youngest daughter, the inn provided safe housing for working women. In 1919, Taft erected the Tudor-style Earls Building at 311 Pike Street to house the director of the Anna Louise Inn and the rector of Christ Church. She also acquired the Greek Revival home at 500 East Fourth Street for the Cincinnati Literary Club and was responsible for the handsome 12-story apartment tower at 506 East Fourth Street, originally known as the Phelps Townhouse and now a hotel.

Even greater was the gift made by her and her husband of the house and invaluable art collection to the people of Cincinnati in 1927, resulting in the public opening of the Taft Museum of Art in 1932. Her father's will stipulated that the Tafts be permitted to occupy the old Sinton homestead on Pike Street as long as they lived.

The Tafts began to collect art seriously in the ear-ly 1900s, and their purchases included European and American master paintings of the 17th through 19th centuries, Chinese porcelains, and European deco-rative arts. Their imposing portraits commissioned from the Spanish painter Raimundo de Madrazo also hang in the museum.

Perhaps the greatest contribution of all, however, was their creation of the Cincinnati Institute of Fine Arts as an instrument to receive the house and art collection on behalf of the city. The Institute was the nation's first community arts fund. Renamed the Fine Arts Fund and now known as ArtsWave, this fund is the largest of its kind in the United States.

—Beth Sullebarger

Nota bene: See also Mary Emery essay on page 9

ALICE WESTON

1926–2019

It's difficult to envision a more enchanted childhood than that of Alice Frieder. Born in Manilla in 1926 to a wealthy cigar exporter and his wife based semi-annually in the Philippine Islands, Weston crossed the Pacific five times before the age of 13.

"We traveled on a wonderful art deco U.S. president line," Weston recalls "That was the most fun I ever had because I could lose my governess and play with the kids." She graduated from Walnut Hills High School and went on to attend Vassar College.

While attending a Christmas party, she spied her future husband, Harris Kempner Weston, whom she would later meet as he exited a tennis court at the Losantiville Country Club. The two married in 1949 and became parents to three daughters.

When their daughter, Barbara, brought a micro-photograph of a cell home from school, Weston was inspired to create her extensive inventory of micro-photographs of crystals. "It looked like a Dubuffet painting that I owned, and it made me want to put everything I could under a microscope to see what it might look like on a larger scale." Weston worked with University of Cincinnati chemist R. Marshall Wilson to create her slides.

In 1971, Weston's work with crystals led to a collaboration with Paul Palombo, head of electronic music at the University of Cincinnati's College-Conservatory of Music (CCM). "Crystal," a 15-minute multi-media composition, premiered at CCM's modern music festival in 1972. "I was lucky to be part of a shift in art that included technology. Where once artists had primarily used paint and canvas, now technology was part of the palette."

Weston was also proud to have inspired the work of a lifelong friend, Pulitzer Prize-winning composer Gunter Schuller. In 1996, *An Arc Ascending* based on Weston's photograph "Winter Solstice"—a picture taken at Fort Ancient Earthworks & Nature Preserve—was performed by Cincinnati Symphony Orchestra.

"Music Hall was completely dark, no light or sound. My annual seasonal calendar, starting with a single winter solstice photo, was phased in and out very slowly…repeated with the spring solstice (and) followed by summer. With all three phased in, and after a brief pause, Gunther's music *An Arc Ascending* began."

Weston amassed a significant art collection based on a discerning purchasing formula. "I've tried to be a discriminating art collector, and I did much of it on a self-imposed budget, traveling to New York at a time when much of the then-contemporary art was new. I patiently ferreted out what was promising and affordable."

She had entered the modern art movement as a college student and insisted on buying early when works were not expensive, and then quickly moved on when a new movement would appear, immediately buying no matter what it was. She never bought art as decoration, only as an investment. "In that way I amassed a very fine art collection very inexpensively."

In addition to being an artist, collector, and muse, Weston (and her husband) endowed the Alice F. and Harris K. Weston Art Gallery at the Aronoff Center for the Arts and a contemporary gallery at the Cincinnati Art Museum. Weston also served on the Art Museum board and its acquisition committee, and the boards of the Contemporary Art Center and American Classical Music Hall of Fame.

—Ilene Ross Tucker

On Sept. 9, 2019, after attending the ArtsWave POWER OF HER luncheon at which she was honored, Alice Weston passed away. Weston's autobiography "Remembering" shares her entire story. The bulk of Weston's art collection, minus pieces gifted to her family, is bequeathed to the Cincinnati Art Museum.

PHYLLIS WESTON

1921–2015

Phyllis Weston is best remembered for her role across five decades as the director of Closson's Art Gallery and proprietor of her own gallery in O'Bryonville, helping local art lovers build their personal collections of paintings and prints.

However, that memory misses the full breadth of her vision.

Growing up in northwestern Ohio, Weston was drawn not just to the visual arts, but also to acting. Though married at 18, and the mother of two young children, she enrolled in acting classes at the Yale School of Drama. During a brief sojourn in Hollywood, she was offered movie roles in films starring Lana Turner and Rita Hayworth, but turned them down, returning to her family on the East Coast. There she befriended Jerome Robbins, George Balanchine, Igor Stravinsky and others in the New York arts scene.

Moving to Cincinnati in 1963, Phyllis quickly discovered the Edgecliff Theatre, landing a part in a Shakespeare production. But when Elizabeth Solway invited her to work at the Solway Gallery, Weston was drawn into gallery work for the first time. A year later, Burton Closson, Jr. hired her to work in his gallery.

For her first show in March 1964, Weston drew on her New York connections, inviting Vera Stravinsky to exhibit her paintings. When Vera and her famous husband, Igor, decided to attend the opening, 2,000 Cincinnatians flocked to the gallery. Over the next 50 years she honed what she considered her great talent to recognize outstanding art.

In addition to bringing nationally and internationally known artists to Cincinnati, Weston showcased local artists, from wildlife artist John Ruthven to abstract expressionist Michael Scott. "I can go from a bird artist to a cutting-edge artist and everything in between," Weston quipped.

Her openness to all styles and periods convinced then-CEO John Smale, in 1981, to hire Weston to assist Procter & Gamble in assembling a corporate art collection focused on Cincinnati artists. For over a decade, Weston searched auction houses and private collections to acquire paintings of well-established nineteenth century painters like, Robert Duncanson and Elizabeth Nourse, and bring their works together with works of twentieth century artists including E.T. Hurley and Jens Jensen. Her great labor became doubly valuable in 2003, when P&G donated 78 paintings by 46 different artists to the Cincinnati Art Museum to form the backbone of new Cincinnati Wing.

Living in Cincinnati for half a century reinforced Phyllis Weston's foundational view that "all the arts are married. You cannot have one without the other." To strengthen Cincinnati's historic commitment to a full spectrum of the arts, she served on the boards of the Contemporary Arts Center, Cincinnati Ballet, and Cincinnati Opera. With Irma Lazarus and Patricia Corbett, she co-founded the Post-Corbett Awards and the Young Friends of the Arts.

It was as if Cincinnati was just waiting for Phyllis Weston to arrive in 1963, soak up its richness, and then help all of us see and appreciate our home in a new way.

—Daniel Hurley

Chapter Two

19TH AND 20TH CENTURY FOUNDERS, LEADERS & CONTEMPORARIES

LAFA / ART ACADEMY OF CINCINNATI (1869)
Sarah Worthington King Peter
Paige Williams
WAMA / CINCINNATI ART MUSEUM (1886)
Elizabeth Williams Perry
Mary Johnston
Alice Bimel
Anita J. Ellis
ARTWORKS (1996)
Tamara Harkavy
BAKER HUNT ARTS & CULTURAL CENTER (1922)
Margaretta Baker-Hunt
CINCINNATI BALLET (1958)
Myrl Laurence, Virginia Garrett and Nancy Bauer
Victoria Morgan
Jennifer Archibald
Heather Britt
Kathy DeLaura
Julie Sunderland
Blanche Maier
Julie Shifman
Ronna Willis
THE CARNEGIE (1974)
Arlene Snyder Gibeau
Sara Vance Waddell
Litsa Spanos
CINCINNATI YOUTH CHOIR (1993)
Robyn Reeves Lana
**COLLEGE-CONSERVATORY OF MUSIC,
UNIVERSITY OF CINCINNATI (1868)**
Clara and Bertha Baur
CONTEMPORARY ARTS CENTER (1939)
Peggy Crawford, Betty Rauh and Rita Cushman
Raphaela Platow
Jennie Rosenthal
Zaha Hadid
CONTEMPORARY DANCE THEATER (1972)
Jefferson James

ENSEMBLE THEATRE CINCINNATI (1986)
Ruth Dennis Sawyer and Mary "Murph" Mahler
D. Lynn Meyers
IT'S COMMONLY JAZZ (1985)
Carolyn Wallace
JUNETEENTH (1988)
Lydia Morgan
Junior League of Cincinnati (1920)
Kentucky Symphony Orchestra (1992)
Angela Williamson
LEARNING THROUGH ART (1992)
Kathy Wade
CINCINNATI MAY FESTIVAL (1873)
Maria Longworth Storer
MUSE CINCINNATI WOMEN'S CHOIR (1984)
Catherine Roma
CINCINNATI MUSEUM CENTER (1990)
Elizabeth Weicher Pierce
Francie Hiltz
CINCINNATI OPERA (1920)
Patricia K. Beggs
Tracy Wilson
CINCINNATI PLAYHOUSE IN THE PARK (1959)
Lois Rosenthal
Ellen van der Horst
KJ Sanchez
CINCINNATI SHAKESPEARE COMPANY (1997)
Marni Penning
CINCINNATI SYMPHONY ORCHESTRA (1895)
Helen Louise "Nellie" Herron Taft
Mary Judge
Sue Friedlander
TAFT MUSEUM OF ART (1927)
Deborah Emont Scott
Vernita Henderson
Sallie Robinson Wadsworth
Woman's Art Club (1892)
Women's Alliance, Inc. (1966)

SARAH WORTHINGTON KING PETER *1800–1877*

Founder of Ladies Academy of Fine Arts and Art Academy of Cincinnati

Cincinnati's society women were at the forefront of the city's movement toward the arts in the mid-19th century. Sarah Worthington King Peter helped take the first steps to earning Cincinnati's reputation as the Athens of the West.

Peter was born into political gentry, the daughter of Thomas Worthington, one of Ohio's first senators and its sixth governor. The family's Adena Mansion in Chillicothe was situated near a Native American burial mound built by the pre-Columbian Adena culture, for which the family's estate was named.

Described as "vigorous, resourceful, possessed of a strong mind and a tender heart," Sarah Peter was an indomitable force for the elevation of women. Although late in life the focus of her generosity shifted to Cincinnati's Catholic charities such as the Sisters of Mercy and the Little Sisters of the Poor, she had an early passion for education and arts.

At the age of 16, she married Edward King, the son of a prominent New York political leader. Eventually the Kings moved from Chillicothe to Cincinnati, where they lived until Edward's death in 1836. Shortly after, she moved to Cambridge, Massachusetts, to be near two of her five children who were attending Harvard University. In 1844, she married William Peter, a British consul to Philadelphia, where she would begin her art philanthropy career.

Starting in 1848, Sarah Peter designated rooms in her home as classrooms for female art students, particularly the social elite, who would work in the decorative arts for the purpose of promoting industry. These classes were the seed that became the Philadelphia School of Design, the first women's art school in the United States, which continues today as the Moore College of Art and Design.

Moving back to Cincinnati in 1853 after her second husband's death, Sarah Peter encouraged the Queen City's budding artists. Her house "became as near an approach to the literary and artistic 'salon' as was seen at that period in America." As her daughter-in-law Margaret Rives King saw it, "Many meritorious artists in music and painting and sculpture owed their success to her inspiration of hope, to her cheering encouragement, and to the still more practical aid which brought to them their support."

In 1854, Sarah Peter founded the Ladies Academy of Fine Arts (LAFA)—also referred to as the Cincinnati Association of Fine Arts—an association of ladies with eighteen members and four officers assembled "to promote interest in art and music … with a view to the improvement of public taste in and the encouragement of art in Cincinnati."

On behalf of the LAFA, Sarah Peter went to Europe with $6,000 to purchase copies of works by old European masters and plaster casts of sculptures, which was the way of art acquisitions for the time. But financial crisis back in Cincinnati left Peter to secure personal loans from friends to pay for artwork already acquired and ready to be shipped home.

With the city's attention and resources fixed on the Civil War, the LAFA disbanded in 1864, and the art collection was bequeathed to the McMicken University then being planned. The plaster casts were used as models for the students of the McMicken School of Design, now the Art Academy of Cincinnati, founded in 1869.

Sarah Peter and her association of collaborating ladies had laid that groundwork.

—Jeff Suess

LAFA Board of Directors

Sarah Worthington King
  Peter, President
Elizabeth H. Appleton
Sarah B. Carlisle
Lucia A. Coleman
Kate L. Davis

Minerva Dominick
Elizabeth H. Hewson
Harriet N. Hosea
Elizabeth Jones
Mary L. Lincoln
C. G. Roelker

PAIGE WILLIAMS

Art Academy of Cincinnati

Paige Williams is passionate about the art she makes and the lives she touches. She found her authentic artistic expression thanks to female role models and mentors. In return, Williams pays it forward by being that role model for her students.

In 2018, Williams was appointed the fifth female dean of the Art Academy of Cincinnati (AAC) in 150 years following in the footsteps of Sarah Colby (1992–95), Jane Stanton (1995–96. Catherine Hardy (2009–10), and Diane Smith (2011–13).

Born in Lexington, Kentucky, Williams earned a BFA from Eastern Kentucky University where she had an all-male faculty. She earned her MFA from the University of Cincinnati where she had one female faculty member. She realized the impact that a male-dominant surrounding had on her and her art. "There was a very masculine kind of pressure. I didn't want my work to look like it was made by a girl or a woman. That is not the case now."

Williams is a painter who also enjoys three-dimensional craft and often works with non-traditional art materials. "My work is non-objective. A lot of my work looks awkward and vulnerable– which is where I think we are most connected. I also think that theme has carried over into my teaching." Representative images from Williams' portfolio are available on her artists' website: *https://paigewilliams.net/home.html*.

In addition to her leadership at the Art Academy of Cincinnati, Williams has taught at Northern Kentucky University in Highland Heights, Kentucky, and the Taft Museum of Art in Cincinnati. She has held visiting artist and lecturer positions at Great Oaks in Cincinnati and University of Michigan. As an Artist in Residence, Williams has pursued her passion for art at the Millay Colony for the Arts in New York, the University of Alaska in Anchorage, the Rathausgalerie in Munich, Germany, and The Vermont Studio Center.

In 2008, Williams received an Ohio Arts Council Individual Excellence Award and a Greater Cincinnati Consortium of Colleges and Universities' Excellence in Teaching Award. Her career at AAC advanced from faculty, to chair of the Master of Arts in Art Education Program, to Chair of the Painting Department. In 2018, Williams was appointed academic dean and says that "the Art Academy has a history of recognizing strong, creative women." Sarah Colby, the college's first female academic dean, was engaging, self-assured, authoritative, prolific, and compassionate. Like Colby, Williams is an educator/artist with a thriving studio practice. "Sarah was a huge mentor and big influence."

Williams embraces the profound influence of the prolific women who, since 1869, have helped shape a revolutionary curriculum to advance women as students, educators, leaders, and influential artists and designers. Maria Longworth Storer, Mary Louise McLaughlin, Elizabeth Nourse, Edie Harper, Constance McClure, Petah Coyne, and Caroline Augusta Lord, are among the many internationally acclaimed female artists who were integral to establishing the Art Academy of Cincinnati as a radical, rebellious college of artists, designers and innovators irrespective of gender.

"I value students where they are, treat them as adults and respect where they're coming from. Our students are fearless, and they inspire me every single day," says Williams. She respects students as unique developing professionals. "Learning is not a one-way street."

—Joan Kaup

ELIZABETH WILLIAMS PERRY *1823–1914*

Founder of Women's Art Museum Association and Cincinnati Art Museum

Elizabeth Williams Perry, a champion of female artists in Cincinnati, was integral to the creation of the Cincinnati Art Museum in 1886. She married Cincinnati attorney Aaron F. Perry, and took a leading role in the city's arts sector.

She began as president of the Women's Centennial Committee, and later as founder and president of the Women's Art Museum Association (WAMA).

Perry formed the Women's Centennial Committee in 1874 "from the common impulse which led similar organizations among women throughout the United States, namely: to secure a creditable representation of women's work at the approaching 'Centennial,' and to bear the expense of its transportation and exposition at Philadelphia." The Cincinnati Room at the Philadelphia Centennial was a huge success.

Invigorated by the response, in 1877 Perry and other members of the Centennial Committee—Sarah B. Carlisle, Mary Shillito, Susan L. Winslow, and Ellen W. Stanwood in particular—formed the Women's Art Museum Association (WAMA). More than 230 women eventually joined WAMA. Their intent was not to fully fund an art museum in Cincinnati, but rather to call out that there ought to be one and advocate for it.

A record of WAMA's history, *A Sketch of the Women's Art Museum Association*, states: "Its object was limited to the effort to awaken and cultivate an interest in the establishment of such an institution, with schools for training in the fine and industrial arts, and thus provide here at home the means which shall raise the general standard of taste, and in time give us our own skilled designers and workmen..."

As the women mobilized to pursue this mission, in January 1878 they wrote to engage prominent attorney Charles P. Taft: "...a museum of the masterpieces of *industrial art* would not be complete without presenting also copies, (or originals) of the masterpieces of art in sculpture and painting...but a leading and controlling idea with the ladies most interested in this movement, is the *industrial* feature of it: to improve the general standard of taste among us; to provide facilities for the improvement of the industries of the county, by showing specimens of the best work done by trained workmen; and by the establishment of technical schools in connection with the Museum, which shall educate in the practice of design, decoration, and other arts and specialties..."

With these guiding principles laid out, WAMA went to work. The women sponsored displays of artwork and handcrafted pieces to raise money and established a selection committee to oversee acquisition of pieces for a permanent museum collection. They established classes in watercolor, china painting, and artistic embroidery. In 1880, Charles W. West gifted $150,000 toward an art museum, contingent on raising a matching amount from the public. An Eden Park location was secured, and the Cincinnati Museum Association was formed to build and operate the museum. Largely pushed out of control in 1884 after seven years of advocacy work, WAMA pivoted its mission to collecting for the museum.

Perry used WAMA's remaining funds to publish the record of their collective efforts from 1877-1886. She lived in Mount Auburn until her death in 1914. Her daughters posthumously published her book, *Studies of A Plant Lover*, in 1921. A portrait of Perry hangs in the permanent collection of the Cincinnati Art Museum.

—Leyla Shokoohe

MARY JOHNSTON *1890–1967*

Cincinnati Art Museum

Mary Elizabeth Johnston is perhaps best known as a modern collector of 19th and 20th century art. Her name graces the collection she generously entrusted through a bequest to the Cincinnati Art Museum.

Perhaps less well known is her close relationship to William Cooper Procter, the second and last member of the founding Procter family to serve as president of the Procter & Gamble Company.

Johnston's father, William Alexander Johnston, was the brother of W.C. Procter's wife, Jane. Johnston lived with her father in the house that he built on Albion Street in Glendale. The Procters had no children of their own, so they doted on their niece like a daughter, encouraging her to be generous in everything she did. The Procters set an example for Johnston through their own generosity to the Christ Church in Glendale, the Episcopal diocese, Children's Hospital, University of Cincinnati, Cincinnati Art Museum, Society of the Transfiguration, and the Widow and Old Men's Home (now Maple Knoll Village), among others.

After Jane Johnston Procter's death in 1953— W.C. Procter had died in 1934—Johnston became heiress to much of the Procter fortune. She was charged with ensuring that the money was spent to benefit the Episcopal Church and "the public in general." Among Johnston's lasting gifts of philanthropy was Procter Hall at the University of Cincinnati College of Nursing.

By then a woman of great adventure and achievement, Johnston was an artist and farmer who tended several residences including her family home in Glendale and a nearby farm. She traveled the world as a battlefield nurse in World War II, a student of innovative educator Maria Montessori in Rome, and a missionary in the Philippines.

And she collected art, a lot of it! She began collecting French Impressionist artists around the time that she served as a nurse in Paris in the mid-1940s. Important works such as van Gogh's *Undergrowth with Two Figures* and Picasso's *Still Life with Glass and Lemon* were on display in her childhood Glendale home. According to Glendale Heritage Preservation, it was well known that Johnston kept her house key under the front doormat while she was traveling. She also loaned her art to museums occasionally, including a 1956 exhibition hosted by the Contemporary Arts Center.

When Johnston died in 1967, her gift of more than thirty 19th and 20th century paintings to the Cincinnati Art Museum became known as The Mary E. Johnston Collection. Johnston's art collection, then valued at $2 million, included paintings of some of her earliest acquisitions by Pablo Picasso and Vincent Van Gogh as well as works by Marc Chagall, Modigliani, Henri Matisse, Paul Cézanne, Piet Mondrian, Georges Henri Rouault, and Max Ernst. *The Mary E. Johnston Collection* was published by Cincinnati Art Museum in 1972.

—Kathy Merchant

ALICE BIMEL *1922–2011*

Cincinnati Art Museum

When Terrie Benjamin began her career at the Cincinnati Art Museum in 1981 as assistant secretary to museum director Millard Rogers, she was shocked to find that Alice Booe Bimel wasn't also receiving a paycheck.

At the time, the museum staff was small, and Rogers relied heavily on volunteers.

As Benjamin recounts, the Asheville, North Carolina, native's role went far beyond the typical part-time docent or general volunteer. "In the first few weeks, I met this woman who came into the office regularly to talk to the director. I didn't really know who she was or why she would come and visit with the director, but I was always impressed by her...(she) clearly had some status in the museum community." Director Rogers would meet with Bimel regularly to talk about museum activities, the docent program and—perhaps most importantly—museum patrons who could benefit the museum financially or donate art collections.

Benjamin's continued reflection on Bimel is that "really she was an unpaid development director. She put in regular hours and she wrote hand-written notes to patrons, inviting them to parties, events, exhibitions, (trying) to get her friends and colleagues interested in the art museum. She was really a wonderful ambassador for the museum."

In 1960, Bimel became a member of the Museum's first docent class, and in 1974 she became the first woman to serve on the Museum's Board of Trustees, paving the way for women to begin serving in high-level capacities throughout the museum system. In her 50+ years as a volunteer, she was a principal asset in assisting with the museum's fundraising efforts before a staffed development department was established in the fall of 1981.

Bimel and her husband, Carl, were avid travelers with keen interests in South Asia, Europe, Greater Iran, and Afghanistan. Significant artworks collected during their travels are now part of the museum's permanent collection, including miniature paintings, a 9th century carved stone pillar from the Pala Dynasty depicting a Serpent King and Queen, and Indian paintings created in the 17th and 18th centuries at the royal Hindu courts of Rajasthan and the Punjab Hills.

In late December 2004, Carl Bimel honored his wife by endowing the museum's Garden Courtyard in her name. "By honoring Alice Bimel, we are not only recognizing the many contributions that she has made to the museum but also celebrating the volunteer spirit that animates this community and has contributed so much to the success of this institution," said Valerie Newell, then-president of the board of trustees.

A landmark gift to the library of $11.75 million in May 2017—which to date is the single most significant monetary gift in the museum's history—established the Alice Bimel Endowment for Asian Art to expand the museum's South Asia, Greater Iran, and Afghanistan collections. At the time, the newly appointed curator of South Asian Art, and Islamic Art and Antiquities, Dr. Ainsley Cameron said, "The opportunity to build an ambitious collection in a public museum today is rare. Alice and Carl Bimel have made that possible for Cincinnati. With this endowment, we can create an exceptional collection, one that represents the vibrancy and vitality prevalent in the arts of the region, from both the historic period and the contemporary."

—Ilene Ross Tucker

ANITA J. ELLIS

Cincinnati Art Museum

When asked to declare a major as an undergraduate, Anita Ellis flipped a coin. Science or art. Without question, Ellis would have devoted herself to either area of study with zeal, inquisitiveness, and perseverance.

Fortunately for Cincinnati, that coin toss determined a career focused on the history and importance of the arts.

Raised in Columbus, Ohio, Ellis developed an appreciation for art through visits to art museums. A full-scholarship student at Ohio Dominican University, Ellis graduated in 1970. Thirty years later, she accepted the college's Distinguished Alumna Award for her contributions to the field of art history and her work toward cultural and civic engagement through the arts.

She continued her art education at various institutions including Cambridge University in England. While completing her master's degree at the University of Cincinnati, Ellis worked in the registrar's office of the Cincinnati Art Museum (1974). Demonstrating great personal initiative and diligence, Ellis was quickly promoted through the ranks, ultimately becoming Curator of Decorative Arts (1981), Director of Curatorial Affairs (1996), Acting Director (1999), and Deputy Director (2007). After 40 years of service and leadership, Ellis retired in 2014.

Ellis's scholarly work and leadership style at the museum were marked by analytical and philosophical rigor. As a curator, Ellis developed deep expertise in all areas of the museum's decorative arts collection (furniture, glass, ceramics, and metals ranging from the Medieval period to the contemporary era). Ellis brought her research and the art museum's collection to national and international attention as the author of numerous books, catalogues, and journal articles, an esteemed lecturer, curator of over fifty exhibition projects, and through transformative art acquisitions.

She became the noted authority on ceramics produced in Cincinnati by The Rookwood Pottery and by Mary Louise McLaughlin, a seminal figure in the history of American ceramics. In 2003, Ellis published the book *The Ceramic Career of M. Louise McLaughlin.*

As the first woman to serve as the director of the museum's curatorial division, Ellis led all curatorial areas to pursue initiatives that would continue to raise the museum's profile. As acting director in 1999, Ellis did not merely "hold down the fort," but generated a renewed momentum for the institution.

During this time, Ellis developed a proposal for a Cincinnati Wing to house a series of 15 galleries showcasing over 400 works of art. It would tell the story of Cincinnati and its people through art and define the city as a great American hub for creativity and artistic production. Opened in May 2003, the Cincinnati Wing represented the first permanent display of a city's art history in the nation, quickly becoming a model for other institutions.

With the same steel and vision held by the ladies of the Women's Art Museum Association who proposed the establishment of the museum for the cultural benefit of the city nearly 125 years prior, Ellis foresaw the potential for Cincinnati's 21st century renaissance and the importance of the museum's role in that movement.

When interviewed in 2000, Ellis stated, "Curatorial work has been so gratifying, allowing me to travel, write, publish and lecture. And, the more I see, the more I envision Cincinnati becoming a major destination city... Our museum is already a medium for that potential. After all, a museum isn't just about our history, it's about our future, who we were, who we are and who we can be."

—Amy Dehan

TAMARA HARKAVY

Founder of ArtWorks

Tamara Harkavy has always colored outside the lines. For this, we can all be grateful. Harkavy is the founder and artistic director of ArtWorks, an organization that began with the idea that public art can change us all.

"We have painted two million feet of wall," Harkavy said. "We deserve beauty in our lives. We deserve inspiration."

Harkavy grew up in North Avondale and went to Walnut Hills High School, then to Arizona State University, before returning home to the University of Cincinnati for a master's in Urban Planning. Her first job was with Downtown Cincinnati, Inc., which emphasized clean, safe streets. Harkavy agreed with the premise, but her idea of what makes a street safe and clean was perhaps more expansive.

The inspiration for ArtWorks was a trip to Chicago to see Gallery 37. In reality, Gallery 37 was just a city block in the Loop, at Dearborn and Randolph streets. It was a singular place for young people to create art. It was truly lovely, but at the time the work was confined to one blighted block.

Harkavy wanted to bring home to Cincinnati the idea of hiring diverse high school students to help make public art. "I was so inspired. I knew I could do this. So, I started this thing which was just a great social experiment."

The idea was to connect talented high school students with working professional artists. The students would be paid fairly, and the artists would be paid too. "Make art, get paid," became a central theme.

ArtWorks has evolved over time. It began in 1996 and 2020 is the program's 25th year of creative existence. All the work is centered around art and beauty, but the program also stresses life skills, budgeting, interviewing for jobs, and discipline. The goal is to help young people, to give them opportunities, to let people believe in themselves, and to do it together. "There was a perception at the time that teenagers together were dangerous," Harkavy said. "I never believed that."

Harkavy is not just ArtWorks. She serves on the board of Ohio Citizens for the Arts, the Art Academy of Cincinnati, Over-the-Rhine Chamber of Commerce, The Mercantile Library, and the 3CDC program committee. She was integral to the creation of Lumenocity and BLINK.

But ArtWorks will be her legacy. There have been more than 100 murals painted in 36 neighborhoods. More importantly, ArtWorks has hired over 3,300 students and 2,900 professional artists since 1996. Friendships have formed, opportunities seized, and lives altered. The byproduct of that mission is that Cincinnati is more beautiful. There are only winners in this equation.

Harkavy has some ideas that can only be described as outrageous. Or audacious. The Ink Your Love project was one of those ideas. She believed the city, her city, could imagine a poem collaboratively, that professional poets could put it down on paper, and that people would then get individual lines from the poem tattooed on their bodies. That all happened.

Harkavy emphasizes collaboration, and how many people have offered their time and money to help. All she wants to talk about is the kids, the young artists who came to discover themselves and make their city more lovely.

"I always thought integrating art and beauty into our neighborhoods would change the street and how we interact with each other. And it kind of has. I am proud of that."

—John Faherty

MARGARETTA BAKER-HUNT *1845–1930*

Founder of Baker Hunt Arts & Cultural Center

Margaretta Baker-Hunt could give lessons on how to turn grief into generosity. In a period of just six years (1888–94), Baker-Hunt lost her only child Katie at age 15 to spinal meningitis. Then, in quick succession, her mother, husband, and father passed.

Such deep family losses might have felled a less sturdy woman. But Baker-Hunt was a visionary leader who was committed to her adopted community of Covington, Kentucky.

Margaretta Baker was born in Cincinnati in 1845 to John and Henrietta Adams Baker. She was named for her paternal grandmother, Margaretta Wager Baker, mother of twelve children including John. Grandfather Baker was a wealthy Philadelphia wine merchant. Music, reading, and religious observance figured prominently in the Bakers' family life. Henrietta Adams was originally from New Hampshire. Her most famous relative, brother John Quincy Adams, was sixth president of the United States.

Stepping back in time, Philadelphia connections and an entrepreneurial spirit figured prominently in shaping the Baker family story. When she married John Baker in 1939, Henrietta Adams Potter was a single mother, widowed for seven years. It was the same year Baker completed an extensive search for a "lively city" to launch a lamp and candle shop with fellow Philadelphian Henry Von Puhl. The Bakers headed to Cincinnati to start a new life chapter.

Although the Baker family moved from Cincinnati to 620 Greenup Street in Covington in 1859, Baker-Hunt continued her education in Cincinnati schools. In 1872, just before her 27th birthday, Margaretta Baker married Dr. William Hunt of Covington. After their daughter Katie died, the Hunts set the stage for a long tradition of philanthropy when they financed a stained-glass window and bell tower at Trinity Episcopal Church.

After Dr. Hunt's passing in 1893, Baker-Hunt never remarried and continued to live in the house at 620 Greenup Street with her globe-trotting niece, Kate Scudder. Miss Scudder (1849–1926) was the daughter of Baker-Hunt's older step-sister, Ann Potter Scudder. The two women became deeply engaged in community activities, opening their home as a meeting place for cultural activities and host-home for associations such as the Linden Grove Cemetery Memorial Association, Covington Culture Club, and Covington Art Club.

With no direct heirs, in 1922 Baker-Hunt formalized her community work by creating the Baker-Hunt Foundation for promotion of art, education, science, psychic research, and good works of religion in the Covington area. She got the idea to use her home in this way from a cousin in the Adams family who had donated a house in New Hampshire for similar purposes. According to Kathryn Witt's book *Secret Cincinnati*, for over thirty years Baker-Hunt used her daughter Katie's room for psychic research and demonstration conducted by Cincinnati medium Laura C. Cooper Pruden.

Today the Art & Cultural Center's campus encompasses nearly three acres of property and four buildings. The house on Greenup Street (built circa 1840) and its surrounding property is the centerpiece. In 1928, shortly before her death, Baker-Hunt laid the cornerstone of a building to house the natural history collection of Archie J. Williams. The museum was disbanded in 1957, but the collection was distributed to Behringer-Crawford Museum and Cincinnati Museum of Natural History & Science. A studio added in 1969 provides a learning space for multiple art media. Completing the campus, in 2000 the Center purchased the house (built circa 1820) that at one time had been Kate Scudder's home.

—Kathy Merchant

CINCINNATI BALLET "BOLD MOVES" (2017)

MYRL LAURENCE, VIRGINIA GARRETT & NANCY BAUER

Founders of Cincinnati Ballet

It was a modest beginning: three middle-aged ballet teachers—Myrl Laurence, Virginia Garrett and Nancy Bauer—sitting in folding chairs in Laurence's Hyde Park studio. The studio was tiny, no more than 500 square feet, but their idea was enormous.

It was 1958, a time when small, semi-professional ballet companies were sprouting up all over the country. Louisville had one. So did Dayton. Even Fort Wayne had a ballet company. Why not Cincinnati?

There were many hurdles they had to overcome on the way to founding the Cincinnati Civic Ballet, which would later morph into the Cincinnati Ballet. There were issues like money and repertory, rehearsal spaces and performance venues.

But the first challenge was to unite the local dance community behind the idea. Dance studios are notoriously competitive businesses. Anything that can possibly pull students away is to be avoided at all cost.

The three founding teachers created an Artistic Council that would guide the direction of the new company. Additionally, they wanted the Council to broaden the geographic diversity of the dancers they hoped to draw from the various studios. Laurence's studio was located in Hyde Park, while Garrett's was in Pleasant Ridge, and Bauer's was in College Hill.

The goal was to recruit the area's busiest and most influential ballet teachers. Soon, they expanded the Artistic Council to include—besides the original three—Shirley Frame Elmore (downtown Cincinnati), Rita O'Neill (Walnut Hills), Dorothy Potts (Deer Park), and Anneliese Von Oettingen (Hyde Park).

It was a formidable group, combining backgrounds on Broadway and European stages and in every aspect of theatrical dance, from tap to modern to—as was the custom of the day—acrobatic and baton twirling.

Their task was daunting. It was one thing to say they wanted to form a ballet company. It was another thing to actually make it happen. How large would the company be, for instance? And who would create the choreography? Where would they rehearse? Should their repertory be built around the classics? Should they include more contemporary works? Most pressing was the question of who should lead the company.

It would take them nearly five years to bring together an ensemble and mount a full-fledged stage production. But as women with their own successful businesses, they knew it was better to take more time and get it right the first time. If they fumbled this first effort, they might not ever have a second chance.

They hired two advanced students as ballet mistresses and brought in Joseph Levinoff, who had danced with the Ballets Russes de Monte Carlo, as artistic advisor.

Finally, on March 31, 1963, they held their first auditions. Two hundred eager youngsters showed up. In the end, just 41 were selected to be part of that inaugural company, which would hold its first performance on March 15, 1964, in the University of Cincinnati's Wilson Auditorium.

—David Lyman

VICTORIA MORGAN

Cincinnati Ballet

As a child growing up in Salt Lake City, Utah, Victoria Morgan was so shy that even the most modest encounter could bring her to tears. Morgan is now artistic director of the Cincinnati Ballet and that long-ago scenario is nearly impossible to imagine.

When you see her stroll self-assuredly onto the stage of the Aronoff Center and welcome thousands of audience members she's anything but shy.

What changed? "Dance," she says. "Dance changed me. It gave me a voice," she told a *Detroit Free Press* reporter in 2002. "I found that I could say things in the studio that I couldn't say anywhere else."

That voice has served her well. She made her first splash at age 12, dancing the leading role of Clara with Ballet West. Five years later, she was in the *corps de ballet* and quickly climbed to principal dancer. Wanting more challenges, she moved to the San Francisco Ballet and, within a few years, was principal dancer there, too.

After stepping away from performing, Morgan spent a decade as resident choreographer and ballet mistress for the San Francisco Opera. She worked extensively with dancers and choreographers. But the position gave her almost no responsibility for dealing with the budgetary or fundraising responsibilities that are the purview of artistic directors.

That didn't seem to be a problem when she interviewed for the artistic director's position at Cincinnati Ballet. "She was a breath of fresh air," search committee member Carol Olson said in *Cincinnati Ballet Celebrates 50*, a book chronicling the company's first half-century. "We had an interesting group of people to choose from. But she stood out. We weren't looking for the same old, same old. We were looking for someone who could shake up the local ballet community."

Morgan not only shook it up, but she did it in ways that broke the cycle of institutional turmoil that defined the decade before she came to Cincinnati. For one thing, she was a female artistic director—still a rarity today, but almost unheard of when she was hired in 1997.

While other companies around the nation folded, she kept Cincinnati Ballet afloat with an ever-more-intriguing repertoire. In 2008, after the company went through four executive directors in less than a decade, Morgan demanded the dual role of artistic director and CEO. Many on the board were aghast. But on April 1, 2008, just as the country plunged into the Great Recession, she got her wish. She soon discovered the company was $800,000 in the red.

Morgan and then-director of finance Craig Lattarulo went to work, reassessing every aspect of spending. Within a year, the company was in the black. "When we got rid of that deficit, it was so liberating," Morgan told the *Cincinnati Enquirer* in 2016. "It meant that we could plan ahead instead of just reacting to bad news. We were in control of our own destiny."

They have done precisely that, vastly expanding the ballet's education and outreach programs and announcing a new home complex. The company has invested in more challenging choreographers and created dozens of fascinating collaborations.

Morgan is now at an age when most people would be looking to retire. Instead, she is planning for the future. "I have enough ballets I want to create and choreographers I want to work with to keep me busy for years to come," she said in a 2017 interview. "So hang on and we'll see what happens."

—David Lyman

JENNIFER ARCHIBALD

Cincinnati Ballet

Jennifer Archibald's choreography wears many faces. Sometimes it is tinged with hip-hop. Other times, modern dance. Or jazz. Or, as some people call it, street dance. She's been Cincinnati Ballet's esteemed resident choreographer since 2017.

The Toronto-born dance-maker meshes all of those styles into the too-often staid world of ballet. Unpredictability is the one thing you can count on from a new Archibald work. And that is precisely what drew Cincinnati Ballet artistic director Victoria Morgan to Archibald in the first place.

When Archibald began making works for the company in 2014, she was an "emerging choreographer." Since then, she's become one of the most prolific and in-demand choreographers in North America. In 2018 alone, she created new works for Cincinnati Ballet, Tulsa Ballet, Grand Rapids Ballet, Amy Seiwert's Imagery, Ballet Nashville, and Stockholm's Balletakademien.

And that is in addition to running her own New York-based Arch Dance Company. She is also a lecturer in acting at Yale School of Drama, has choreographed several off-Broadway and regional musicals, new works for more than 20 colleges and universities, and commercials for Nike, Tommy Hilfiger and MAC Cosmetics.

Her appeal? Consistently, Archibald's movement is as visually appealing to audiences as it is challenging to the dancers. Then there is the chameleon-like stylistic breadth of her choreography itself. Where some choreographers' work is so distinctive that it is easy to spot, the eclectic nature of Archibald's movement means that seeing her work is always an adventure. Sometimes, it is "pure" movement, with no attendant storyline. But other dances have a hint of a narrative—about love, about the complexity of friendships, about the dance itself.

She is regarded as "a dancer's choreographer" —a generous creator who cherishes the performers who work with her and finds satisfaction in crafting movements that fit their strengths. In the studio, she is known for her intensity and for her ability to work quickly. Spend any time in Archibald's studio and you're sure to hear an oft-repeated mantra: "Go hard or go home."

—David Lyman

HEATHER BRITT

Cincinnati Ballet

Raised on Cincinnati's West Side, Heather Britt began her dance training at the age of three, studying everything the teachers at the Dance Artist studio could offer her: ballet, tap, jazz, and acrobatic.

In fourth grade, she transferred from the French-immersion program at Midway Elementary to the School for Creative and Performing Arts (SCPA).

At SCPA, she was exposed to a vast range of dance styles—including Martha Graham modern dance technique and West African dance—drama, and a rich community of like-minded creatives.

After briefly attending college in Colorado, she abandoned dance altogether. As she explained it, there simply didn't seem to be a place in the dance world where she fit in. But a summer job teaching ballet at the French Woods Festival of the Performing Arts in Hancock, New York, rekindled her enthusiasm for dance, if not for ballet.

She moved to San Francisco and hurled herself into African dance and the Bay Area's adventurous modern dance scene. She also got involved with a group called Rhythm & Motion, whose high-energy dance classes combined a mesmerizing mix of exercise and artistry.

Eventually, Britt returned to Cincinnati, launched a Midwest outpost of the Rhythm & Motion franchise, and became Cincinnati Ballet's education director. That gave her access to Cincinnati Ballet's largest studio for her popular Rhythm & Motion classes.

Ballet artistic director Victoria Morgan was fascinated with Britt's enthusiasm in the studio. In 2009, she asked Britt to create a piece for the company's New Works series. Many regarded it as a gamble, both for the Ballet and for Britt. But, in retrospect, said the *Cincinnati Enquirer*, "Britt's raw, robust choreography has unleashed a side of the dancers that audiences rarely get to see."

Britt joined the faculty at Northern Kentucky University and Uptown Arts, while continuing to create at least one new piece of choreography for Cincinnati Ballet every year. In 2014 Britt launched DANCEFIX by HBDC (Heather Britt Dance Company).

—David Lyman

KATHY DELAURA

Cincinnati Ballet

Today, we know Kathy DeLaura as a savvy strategic planner and an ingenious fundraiser. She's the woman with a plan.

As managing director of Partners in Change, she has many long-term clients who can attest to that.

But over the course of her long career, she has worn many hats. She was the first executive director and COO of the national Speaking of Women's Health foundation and executive director of the Cincinnati Foundation for Biomedical Research and Education at the VA Medical Center. She is also the board president of Ensemble Theatre Cincinnati.

But rarely in her career did she face challenges quite so daunting as she did during the two separate periods she worked with Cincinnati Ballet.

The first was in 1985. She began less than four months after the death of the company's long-time artistic director, David McLain. Though she was there just 14 months, she shepherded the company through a time of uncertainty and secured a new artistic director, former American Ballet Theatre superstar, Ivan Nagy.

Her second stint, from 1990 to 1997, was even more eventful. As she recalls, "They asked me to come back and save the Ballet and I took it very seriously." It was a turbulent time. Nagy and his executive director had suddenly exited the Ballet leaving a $1 million deficit. The new artistic director, ballet master Richard Collins, was killed in an auto accident just 10 months after DeLaura returned.

Working with the Cincinnati Opera's Gus Stuhlreyer, who had been hired to oversee finances, DeLaura and new artistic director, Nigel Burgoine, devised ingenious and inventive ways to bring an audience back to the company. Not only did their imaginative ideas succeed, but by the time DeLaura left in late 1997 as artistic director Victoria Morgan was joining the Ballet, the company was on a healthy economic path.

JULIE SUNDERLAND

Cincinnati Ballet

Born in Brooklyn, Sunderland came to Cincinnati at age eight. At first, she loathed her new city.

"I grew up in a neighborhood and family filled with sarcastic people," she says. "The Midwest was all about being nice. I didn't get it."

She attended several high schools before graduating from Wayland Academy in northern Wisconsin. She began college at Northland College where she studied the Ojibway language, among other academic intrigues. But the fit wasn't right. She tried acting in Chicago—she was great at improv—and worked in Santa Cruz before landing back in Cincinnati.

Surprisingly, her breakthrough job was as a server at Mitchell's Fish Market restaurant. Her enthusiasm and boundless energy made her such a stand-out that a manager asked her to become a trainer. It proved to be a perfect position, taking full advantage of her strongest qualities.

Inspired by DANCEFIX classes, she began teaching movement to incarcerated teens. In 2008, she became Cincinnati Ballet's education director and later, the company's vice-president of community and inclusion.

For more than 10 years, she was the face of the company's outreach programs, championing dance for anyone anywhere—jazzy dance routines in Washington Park, dance classes for kids with disabilities.

Sunderland left Cincinnati Ballet in August 2019, though she continues to teach Ballet Moves classes geared to children and young adults with a variety of disabilities. She also teaches classes for special needs children in schools around the area.

Sunderland is a founding member of the Greater Cincinnati Access and Inclusion Network, which is dedicated to making all aspects of the community more inclusive for people with disabilities. "Dance connects people," says Sunderland. "It connects people in ways that almost nothing else does. *That's* why I do this. It's all about creating communities."

—David Lyman

BLANCHE MAIER *1927–2009*

Cincinnati Ballet

Family was everything to Blanche. Monday evening family dinners were generous affairs, spirited and enormous.

To her, family wasn't just a matter of genes. It was about friendship and fostering a sense of community.

It's no coincidence that those were qualities that came to define the family business, Frisch's Restaurants. The chain of family restaurants was founded in 1939 by Maier's father, David Frisch and later led by the man she married in 1949, Jack Maier. After David Frisch's death in 1970, the couple continued working together to grow Frisch's into a major regional force.

Maier's commitment to community kept her involved with a wide range of organizations, from the Springer School and the Greater Cincinnati Charity Horse Show to the Cincinnati Country Day School. But her greatest passion was for the Cincinnati Ballet, where she volunteered from the company's earliest days. She would go on to serve as board president from 1989 to 1992 and served two terms as board chair. She would remain an emeritus trustee until her death in 2009.

Her enthusiasm for Cincinnati Ballet led to Frisch's becoming the lead underwriter for the company's production of *Nutcracker*. That was 1974. In one of the area's most enduring corporate arts sponsorships, Frisch's has remained the production's primary sponsor ever since.

So deep was Maier's dedication to the company that when Victoria Morgan created a new production of *Frisch's Presents The Nutcracker* in 2011, she named the opening scene, in which characters are preparing for a holiday party, "Blanche's Kitchen."

JULIE SHIFMAN

Cincinnati Ballet

Victoria Morgan had already planned to take Cincinnati Ballet to New York when she noticed an opportunity.

The Cincinnati Symphony Orchestra and May Festival had performances there the following week.

Surely, she thought, there must be some way to spin these events to generate a more significant promotional splash. So she called Ballet board member Julie Shifman, a former partner with Thompson Hine and a successful serial entrepreneur. She was sure that Julie would have some good ideas. She couldn't have been more right.

Shifman named the 2014 campaign "Cincy in NYC." Before long, she had recruited Cincinnati Opera, Taft Museum of Art, Cincinnati Art Museum, Playhouse in the Park, and the College-Conservatory of Music, along with dozens of corporations, executives and politicians, in a sprawling showcase of all things Cincinnati. Cincinnati was everywhere, from gallery exhibitions and Cincinnati-themed gatherings in some of the city's hippest downtown clubs to an extraordinary seven-course dinner hosted by Cincinnati culinary luminaries at the James Beard House.

No one who knew Shifman was surprised. Even before the New York project, Shifman was deeply involved in the civic life around her. She'd been the board chair at Talbert House, and a trustee of Hebrew Union College, United Way, YWCA, and the American Jewish Committee.

In 2008, she had launched a company she called Act Three, with the mission to assist former professional women trying to re-enter the work force after stepping away to raise families. That led to a successful career as an author and inspirational speaker. Most recently, she became the executive director of Adopt A Class, a group that fosters relationships between business professionals and area schools. Under her leadership, the group has grown to more than 2,500 volunteers serving more than 6,000 students a month.

—David Lyman

RONNA WILLIS

Cincinnati Ballet

Though Ronna Willis has supported many of Cincinnati's arts institutions, including Playhouse in the Park, Cincinnati Opera, the Cincinnati Symphony Orchestra, and Ensemble Theatre Cincinnati, she is best known for her long-time work with the Cincinnati Ballet.

Drawn to the Ballet by her history as a dancer, she has served in many capacities, including as a trustee for 20 years and the chair of several committees.

Willis is the type of person to not only recognize a problem, but to roll up her sleeves and solve it. When she noticed that Cincinnati Ballet's dancers were missing an advocate at the board level, she helped to form the TLC Committee (now the Dancer Relations and Communications Committee), which took on tasks such as arranging meals for dancers when they spent the entire day in the studio. Feeding the dancers came down to more than money; it made better use of rehearsal time as the dancers' muscles didn't cool down and they could waste less time traveling. Willis arranged for board members to cook and bring in food, which also nurtured relations between the two groups.

Willis' compassionate problem-solving didn't stop with the TLC Committee. "Most of the professional dancers don't get to go to college," Willis explains. "I thought there was a real need for dancers to become more educated." This seed of an idea became Beyond Ballet, a program to bolster dancers preparing to make career transitions. Willis helped to initially fund Beyond Ballet and arranged for a Cincinnati State professor to visit the studio after rehearsals to offer a college course, making the process as easy as possible for the dancers. "I had students who graduated college because of that start," Willis recalls.

Willis has been called the fairy godmother of the Ballet because of supportive, behind-the-scenes initiatives such as these, but she is also capable of taking the spotlight—in fact, Willis has performed several on-stage roles with the Ballet. "I love being part of the Ballet productions, it really lets me get to know the dancers up close and personal," she says. These are no small cameos, either—Willis portrayed the Grandmother in *The Nutcracker*; Auntie Annie in Victoria Morgan's new *Nutcracker*; Hippolyta in *A Midsummer Night's Dream*; the Queen in *Swan Lake*; and the Fortune Teller in *Don Quixote*.

Willis' on-stage experience with the Ballet led to a similar invitation from Cincinnati Opera, for which she has performed roles in *Der Rosenkavalier*, *Tosca*, and *Madama Butterfly* (sharing the stage with her own 4- and 6-year-old grandsons, a fond memory for Willis). "This summer (of 2019) was my favorite role of all with the Opera. I was Lady Capulet in *Romeo and Juliet*," she says with a laugh. "I had to collapse on stage... it was a really great role."

Cincinnati's arts scene has been deeply nurtured by the blend of loving stewardship and bright passion that Ronna Willis brings with her. "I have been paid back so many times," she insists. "I have loved helping all of these companies."

—Erica Reid

ARLENE SNYDER GIBEAU *1923–2012*

Founding Director of The Carnegie

Covington Public Library was built in 1904. Industrialist and philanthropist, Andrew Carnegie spent $60 million—nearly $2 billion in today's dollars—to build 1,700 public libraries across the United States (1883 to 1929), including Covington's Beaux Arts building.

Despite earning a spot on the Register of Historic Places in 1971, by winter 1974 the building needed extreme repair and renovation. The City of Covington didn't have the resources to bring the building back to life and was prepared to tear it down.

But never underestimate the passion and power of civic leaders to save an historic building! A group of Covington residents formed the Northern Kentucky Arts Council (NKAC). Becoming the building's only tenant, and armed with a vision to create an arts center, the volunteers of NKAC kept this vision alive for nearly a decade before they had enough money to hire staff. In 1983, Arlene Gibeau "worked for next to nothing" according to Aileen May, one of the original NKAC trustees. "She mounted cutting-edge shows on a shoestring," often as a volunteer because meeting payroll was not guaranteed.

Experienced in managing arts programming at the Kenton County Cooperative Extension, Arlene was described as an arts activist "whose gracious manners concealed the energy of a titan." She faced the daunting task of raising money for arts programming and finding the resources needed to restore the structure and keep it heated. The Kenton County Historical Society reported that Arlene "stepped into this dismal picture with positive energy and enthusiasm. She was described as emanating 'sparks of magic.'"

Early in Arlene's tenure, two events provided the means to develop a comprehensive Carnegie Visual and Performing Arts Center to provide arts education, exhibition galleries, and live theater. In 1985, the Fine Arts Fund (now ArtsWave) launched the first Northern Kentucky fund drive. Rather than going it alone, the Carnegie Center helped raise money and became a beneficiary.

That relationship helped to address the programming challenge. Several years later, a surprise $100,000 bequest from a Covington philanthropist meant that Arlene could excavate and revitalize the old theater. It had been sitting derelict in the heart of the building since 1958.

In honor of her leadership, and her commitment to supporting local artists and arts promotion, Arlene Gibeau received the 1992 Post-Corbett Award. She retired in 1996, the same year The Carnegie celebrated its silver (25th) anniversary as an historic icon.

By then it was clear that The Carnegie could stand up on its own. The following year, in 1997, the board of the Northern Kentucky Arts Council took an important step to integrate the brand identity of the organization with the facility. The State of Kentucky granted a DBA (doing business as) certificate which effectively ended the confusion caused by using two names for one entity.

As the 21st century dawned, The Carnegie launched a complete renovation, including several additions to the footprint during 2001–03. Northern Kentucky philanthropist Eva Farris donated funding to establish an education center in 2004. In the years that followed, grants from the Otto M. Budig Family Foundation and gifts from hundreds of donors supported full renovation of the theater and glass ceiling dome.

Today, The Carnegie (as it's now known for short) is a robust organization, the only multidisciplinary arts venue in Northern Kentucky, still anchored in its founding platform of education, galleries, and theater.
—Kathy Merchant

SARA VANCE WADDELL

The Carnegie

Arts philanthropist, board member, collector, and project-organizer extraordinaire, Sara Vance Waddell is a powerful agent for progressive change in the art world. Recently in an interview, she discussed her opinions on the current state of gender equity in the arts.

She takes pride in the work she's done for The Carnegie Visual and Performing Arts Board of Directors over nearly a decade.

Amassing one of the largest collections of female artists in the Midwest—featuring local and internationally recognized artists—Vance Waddell frequently loans artworks from her collection to institutions around the world. She believes that meaningful art should be on view and accessible to the public as much as possible.

Vance Waddell serves as a catalyst for positive change on several boards, including (but not limited to,) the Ohio Advisory Group and National Advisory Board for the National Museum of Women in the Arts, and the Modern Women's Fund Committee of the Museum of Modern Art in New York. During her tenure at The Carnegie, she held board officer positions of secretary, vice president, and president.

Over the past nine years that she has been part of The Carnegie's board, Vance Waddell says she is most proud of leaving the organization better than she found it. Under her leadership, The Carnegie hired a new executive director, and she co-chaired the organization's capital campaign for the building and educational improvements that were launched in 2019.

But Vance Waddell is in it for the long haul. She realizes that the work of affecting positive social change doesn't happen overnight.

When asked what her experience as an arts' advocate has taught her about supporting women in the arts, Vance Waddell doesn't waste a second replying with gravitas: "We have a tremendous lot of work to do."

Vance Waddell collects primarily the art of women of color, as well as local Cincinnati artists. "I think it's really important to support local artists. We have so many good ones—why aren't more collectors supporting them?" she wonders with a measure of disbelief.

To that aim, she co-founded programs like *The Art of She* at The Carnegie, which was founded to promote local women artists, support the Carnegie's gallery programs, and help people acquire work by women artists, both emerging and established.

The Carnegie is not Vance Waddell's only community passion, however. She has previously served on boards for the Ronald McDonald House, Cincinnati Art Museum, and Contemporary Arts Center. She is an Honorary Lifetime Trustee of Cancer Family Care and Living with Change.

In all of her work, Vance Waddell strives to support Cincinnati's art scene in the spotlight of her national and international connections and collections. "I'm never going to stop supporting my local community—that's just never going to happen," she says determinedly. "If my reach becomes broader than just local, then that's a good thing."

—Maria Seda-Reeder

LITSA SPANOS

The Carnegie

Litsa Spanos knew more than 25 years ago that she had a true passion for what she now does every day: sell art as the founder of Art Design Consultants, Inc. Her inspiration springs from a deep commitment to promote the work of artists.

She creates a sense of community among artists and art lovers.

Spanos has always loved art and design, even as a young girl. "One of the reasons I entered the art world and made it a career is because of my love of original artwork," says Spanos. "Nothing inspires me like art. Why? Art is a true labor of love. I knew that if I felt this way about the power of art, others would have this reaction as well."

Spanos' favorite quote is by sociologist Charles Horton Cooley who created the "looking glass" theory of human connection: "An artist cannot fail; it is a success to be one." That is not to say that artists won't need a little help to be successful. That's where Litsa Spanos comes in.

Right after college, Spanos' first job was working in an art gallery. The next step was to launch her own art consultant business "and I've never looked back." Spanos' mission is to make artwork more accessible to individuals and companies, and to help elevate artists to more successful careers.

About ten years ago, Spanos experienced a burst of her own creativity that took several forms. One was to become involved in two arts organizations. "I first got involved with The Carnegie and the Opera because of each organization's ability to lift you up beyond everyday experiences." As an example of how Spanos encouraged the organizations to get more deeply connected in the community, in 2016 she helped to found and co-chaired an event at The Carnegie called the "Art of She." A series of creative events inviting the community to connect with and champion women artists and leaders (and raise money for programming at The Carnegie).

Around that same time, Spanos created what has become a signature event for her company, artists, and this community. The idea for *Art Comes Alive* came from one of Cincinnati's many luncheon events honoring business leadership. Spanos thought "Why can't artists be recognized in this same way? They work hard, persevere through hardships, and make outstanding contributions to our community."

What began as a simple idea to celebrate artists in Cincinnati soon grew to national heights. In just one decade, *Art Comes Alive* has recognized and supported over 1,500 artists across the country, sold over 400 works of art, and awarded more than $1.9 million in sales, contracts and cash prizes for those artists.

During the last five years, Spanos has also expanded her horizons as an author to complement the mentoring and coaching she provides to individual artists as they develop their careers. *Secrets of the Art World: Getting Real About the Process, Business and Selling of Your Work* helps creatives with the practical aspects of turning artistic talent into business success.

Throughout her career in the arts as well as in her life, Spanos says that dreaming big and not being afraid to take risks have been central to her success: "I truly believe if you have the passion and perseverance, then you can accomplish anything."

—Kathy Merchant

ROBYN REEVES LANA

Founder of Cincinnati Youth Choir

Robyn Reeves Lana teaches music. Yes, hit the right note, make sure the diction and intonation are on point. But more is happening than often meets the ear. As the 1993 founder and artistic director of the Cincinnati Youth Choir, Reeves Lana makes an impact.

She doesn't waste her yearly access to about 1,000 children in first through 12th grades to teach them life lessons and help them to further understand their complicated world.

"I want them to get lost in the music, to escape from the strife and pressure," she said on an unseasonably hot, humid Thursday afternoon backstage at the College-Conservatory of Music (CCM) at the University of Cincinnati. "Kids today have more baggage than we had. They can explain their feelings and happenings as they explore vocal music."

She carried seven mid-size plastic bins and lids into the rehearsal room, one for each of her seven choirs-in-residence at the conservatory. Her singers deposit their cell phones in the bins before rehearsal and can retrieve them 90 minutes later when finished.

Reeves Lana also selects topical pieces for her students. One of her choirs, Bel Canto, is rehearsing "A Hive of Frightened Bees," a poem written by a Colorado high school student and set to music by composer Andrea Reeves. The piece addresses students' fears of growing up in the age of widespread school shootings. Another choir, Voci Sopra, a high school treble group, is working on "Song of Hope," a spiritual that also addresses troubles in the world.

"Music is the best tool for feeling everything else," Reeves Lana said. "It's what we use to help them become better citizens of the world, nicer to each other, and more accepting of differences."

Reeves Lana knows first-hand the power of music. A Connecticut native, she earned her bachelor's (1987) and master's (1991) degrees in music education from CCM. Her list of workshops and guest appearances as a conductor and clinician stretches three pages on her curriculum vitae. What her CV doesn't show is the life lesson she began teaching her singers in 2018.

Vision loss in one eye and reduced vision in the other ultimately revealed two brain aneurysms. She sought treatment at Mayo Clinic in Rochester, Minnesota. She lived because they didn't burst. Back in Cincinnati, assistants had to take over conducting the choirs. She didn't hide her conditions or the effects of medicine from her students. Steroids caused hair loss. As she healed through winter and spring 2019, though, Reeves Lana grew physically strong enough to attend rehearsals.

"When I heard them sing, I would sit there and cry," she said.

She exchanged calls and text messages with a choir member who had battled and defeated a brain tumor. Reeves Lana drew strength from the young woman, whom she called "one of my biggest shoulders." Another life lesson taught and learned through music. She let her students in close enough to help her. They rose to the challenge.

"I could see it," she said, "the love in their eyes."

—Mark Curnutte

CLARA BAUR *1835–1912*

BERTHA BAUR *d. 1940*

Founders of the University of Cincinnati College-Conservatory of Music

There are those who exhibit such unwavering dedication that they create a legacy lasting for centuries. Such is the life work of Clara Baur, founder of the Cincinnati Conservatory of Music, and her niece Bertha Baur, assistant and later president.

Clara was born in Stuttgart, Germany, in 1835. At age 13, she joined her brothers in Cincinnati and found herself in a city with a burgeoning arts community. It was in this environment that Clara's love of music—combined with an entrepreneurial spirit—took root and flourished.

In her early 30s she, like many musicians of the day, returned to Europe to study and deepen her skills among the world's greats. But in 1867, her purpose grew larger: establish a music conservatory with a first-rate faculty.

Clara returned to Cincinnati, and within a year the Cincinnati Conservatory of Music was born. With three faculty members working in a rented room in Miss Nourse's School for Young Ladies, she established one of the first music conservatories in the United States (and possibly the first residential conservatory in the country).

Many called her conservatory "The Nursery" because most of her students were daughters of Cincinnati's elite. How they underestimated Clara's strong determination to build a lasting, quality program. She turned it into an internationally recognized educational institution that included a full music curriculum and a placement bureau to help graduates find employment. In less than 20 years, the faculty grew to 23. By 1902 she had nearly 1,000 students.

A natural networker, Clara attracted renowned musicians from around the world to teach. Adept at fostering support in the community, she offered open performances for the public, classes for music appreciation for children, and continuing education for adults.

She also collaborated with the Cincinnati Symphony Orchestra, guaranteeing a post for the concertmaster and teaching opportunities for orchestra musicians. This insight helped ensure that quality musicians stayed in the community and became outstanding teachers for the Conservatory.

Clara was not alone in her devotion to the Conservatory. In 1867, she wisely recruited her niece, Bertha Baur, from Michigan to join her as an assistant. This proved a life-long career for Bertha who stood by Clara's side as they weathered the challenges and savored the opportunities in building a prestigious music conservatory over the decades.

Clara passed away in 1912 at the age of 77. Upon her aunt's passing, Bertha assumed the role of director of the Conservatory. By 1930, she had turned it over to the Cincinnati Institute of Fine Arts, making it a non-profit organization. Bertha then retired and was named president emeritus until her death in 1940.

Together, Clara and Bertha made a significant impact on the musical culture of Cincinnati and the country. *The 1906 World Almanac Book of Facts* wrote, "Miss Baur's direction widened its circle of influence until there is not a state today that has not profited by the culture of its graduates… The Cincinnati Conservatory of Music has played a significant part in the development of musical culture in America."

And, it continues. In 1962 the Conservatory merged into the Cincinnati College of Music to become the 14th college at the University of Cincinnati, now called the College-Conservatory of Music (CCM).

—Susan Fellows Crabtree

PEGGY CRAWFORD, BETTY RAUH, & RITA CUSHMAN

Founders of Contemporary Arts Center

The Contemporary Arts Center's (CAC) 1979 exhibition, *The Modern Art Society: The Center's Early Years 1939–54*, gave the fledgling museum a chance to look back at its foundational years when it was known as the Cincinnati Modern Art Society.

Fortunately for the CAC then, and for us now, the Society's three founders—Peggy Frank Crawford, Betty Pollak Rauh, and Rita Rentschler Cushman—were able to contribute essays to the catalogue for the show curated by Ruth Meyer. They knew by then that they had changed—modernized—Cincinnati's art world forever, bringing the city's art world into the 20th century. We have never turned back.

"'Modern Art' sounds old-fashioned today, and 'Society' slightly 19th century," Cushman wrote in 1979. "But in 1939 these were brave words, evoking in some Cincinnatians a disapproval normally reserved for nudism, free sex or bare feet in the kitchen."

In 1939, Peggy Frank and Betty Pollak were recent graduates of Smith and Wheaton, respectively, with a keen interest in art. After Pollak broke her leg skiing, family friend Edward Warburg visited her. As he was a trustee of New York's Museum of Modern Art (MoMA), Pollak and Frank asked him about art-world jobs in New York. He suggested they start something in Cincinnati instead, and they decided to try. Frank brought in Cushman, a married young woman she knew from Art Academy of Cincinnati classes. (Pollak married Morton Rauh that same year.)

The Modern Art Society raised $5,000 in just a few weeks to stage its first six exhibitions at Cincinnati Art Museum (CAM), which allowed use of its galleries. Gifts were limited to $100 to broaden community support. Warburg and MoMA director Alfred Barr, Jr., sat on the advisory board, as did CAM Director Walter Siple.

Frank became the Society's director and immediately began planning shows that borrowed from local and national collections. Her first show, *Exhi-*

bitions of Modern Paintings from Cincinnati Collections, opened in November 1939. The next year, she brought several important shows to town, including *Picasso—40 Years of His Life*, that featured his then-new masterpiece *Guernica*.

In 1940, Frank took a class at the Art Academy from renowned American modernist painter Ralston Crawford. In 1942, they married and left Cincinnati. She eventually developed an active and much-honored career as a photographer.

In 1952, the Modern Art Society moved into renovated space at the Art Museum, and subsequently became the Contemporary Arts Center (CAC). In the 1960s, it started staging exhibits elsewhere. In 1970, CAC moved to its first dedicated home, leased space in a Downtown building. In 2003, it opened its first freestanding building, designed by the Iraqi-born British architect Zaha Hadid. It was the first U.S. museum designed by a woman.

Crawford chose to close her essay for that 1979 CAC exhibit by looking forward rather than back: "Who knows what child in Corryville coming here next week may become Cincinnati's Duveneck of the 21st century because the Cincinnati Modern Art Society held its first show in 1939?"

Rita Rentschler Cushman died in 1994, Betty Pollak Rauh in 2001, and Peggy Crawford in 2015. Upon Crawford's passing, CAC Director Raphaela Platow said that, as the first director, Crawford had started the Society "against all odds, in a moment of time when the Great Depression was still shaking the world and the Second World War was about to erupt." And it still continues strong.

—Steven Rosen

RAPHAELA PLATOW

Contemporary Arts Center

When Raphaela Platow was approached about becoming the director of the Contemporary Arts Center (CAC) in 2007, friends' reactions were universal. "They thought I was crazy," she recalled. "How could I possibly go there?"

After all, the CAC was the epicenter of the controversy over Robert Mapplethorpe's gorgeous and graphic photos. It was the place where both the museum and its then-director, Dennis Barrie, had been charged with pandering obscenity and subjected to an internationally notorious trial.

Platow, on the other hand, was an up-and-coming art world star. Educated in Berlin, Freiburg, and at the Sorbonne, she'd been part of the German pavilion team at the 1999 Venice Biennale and had most recently been acting director and chief curator at Brandeis University's Rose Art Museum. Why leave the hallowed ground of east coast art to go to the Midwest? And to an institution that had been sullied on the world stage?

"I think I'm an ultimate risk taker," says Platow, now the museum's Alice & Harris Weston Director and Chief Curator. "I love challenges and figuring out how to overcome them. I think I'm also a good diplomat." Besides, she was inheriting an institution housed in a famed Zaha Hadid-designed structure in the center of the city.

There was much to build on. But there would definitely be bumps along the way. Struck by the emotional chill of the CAC's first floor, she proposed turning it into a more inviting space. It was the CAC space most visible to the world outside.

The very idea that she would tinker with what some people consider an architectural masterpiece unleashed a torrent of outrage from some corners, including Hadid. She wrote a blistering letter to Richard Rosenthal, one of the building's lead sponsors, saying how embarrassed she was by the changes they'd made and likening the new look to the lobby of a chain hotel.

On the record, at least, Platow avoided the fray, saying that "The CAC is a beautiful place. It's a sophisticated place and an artful space. Now it's also a welcoming place."

She and her staff have developed robust programs for teenagers and young adults, a rarity in museum circles. She has reinvigorated—some might say reinvented—the museum's once-vaunted performing arts program.

Most important, she has pursued a sense of community befitting a building occupying such a central location in the city.

"We have the most diverse audiences here," says Platow. "And that is what I've spent my life trying to do, to take down—literally—the metaphorical columns that we so often build up between ourselves and the people we are here to serve. Now, I think we can truly regard what Zaha Hadid created as an urban carpet."

—David Lyman

JENNIE ROSENTHAL

Contemporary Arts Center

"Service *does* begin at home," says Jennie Rosenthal. "And for me, it was a way of life." The daughter of two renowned Cincinnati philanthropists, Richard and Lois Rosenthal, she was explaining how she came to her own life of philanthropy and public service.

"My brother and I grew up in a family where empathy and caring about the world around you was important," says Rosenthal. "That's where we learned how life was supposed to be lived." Clearly, she has followed that path, from serving as the board president of the Contemporary Arts Center (CAC) to being chair of the National Planned Parenthood Action Fund Board.

Some might regard her CAC leadership as destiny. After all, her parents were the lead donors for the CAC's Zaha Hadid-designed home in the center of downtown Cincinnati, officially named the Lois & Richard Rosenthal Center for Contemporary Art.

"From the outset, what drew me to the Contemporary Arts Center (CAC) was how personal the arts I saw there were. It was never about showing the hottest or the trendiest artists. It was about the personal connections that people could make with it."

But it was more than that. It was the CAC's defining philosophy that enticed Rosenthal to become a board member in 1993. "What excited me so much was the organization's commitment to not just showing exhibits of artists, but to developing relationships with them."

There was also an institutional hunger to share those relationships with the public that Rosenthal continued to champion when she moved into a leadership role. "I strongly believed—and I still do—that we should stretch our mission of educating people, of creating active programs for kids, and building a robust docent population. You have to give the community a way of learning about it and also exploring it."

It was an attitude that was fostered not just at home and in community work, but in her career, too.

From the time she was a child, her goal was to work at F&W Publications, the family publishing business. On July 1, 1985, that wish came true and she became the fifth generation of her family to enter the business, growing a business that focused on books and magazines that revolved around the work of writers, visual artists and craftspeople.

In time, she took on a host of executive positions and became the first woman on the company's executive committee. But when the business was sold in December 1999, she was uncertain where to turn her energy.

That gave her the opportunity to pour her efforts more deeply into the CAC and a number of other groups as she joined the board of Seven Hills School and the YWCA. Later, she would become a powerhouse fundraiser for the Democratic Party, both locally and nationally, as well as an executive committee member for the Ohio Innocence Project.

In the ensuing years, her public involvement has been wide-reaching and varied. In addition to being an emeritus trustee of the CAC and a leader in the national Planned Parenthood organization, she is a member of the Global Advisory Council of the Wilson Center in Washington, D.C., and has served on the boards of Playhouse in the Park, Findlay Market, the Teton Valley Ranch Camp of Jackson Hole, Wyoming, the University of Cincinnati Rowing Alumni Association, and the Greater Cincinnati Foundation's community investment committee.

—David Lyman

ZAHA HADID *1950–2016*

Contemporary Arts Center

Born in Baghdad, educated in London and Switzerland, architect Zaha Hadid had a remarkable, if too-short, career of firsts. The first woman to receive the Pritzker Architecture Prize which is thought of as the Nobel Prize of architecture.

She was also the first woman to be awarded the Royal Gold Medal from the Royal Institute of British Architects. The list goes on and on.

In life, she had a reputation as a demanding and often difficult employer. But then, she had her own vision of what buildings—and life itself—should and could be. When asked to describe the goals of good architecture, Hadid had a simple answer, one that very clearly described her vision. "It should feed the soul," she said. "And it should keep you dry."

At her graduation from London's Architectural Association School of Architecture, one of her most distinguished professors, Dutch architect Rem Koolhaas described her as "a planet in her own orbit."

Her vision was so singular that, early in her career, she had far more designs that failed to be built than projects that were actually completed.

But in 2003, with the opening of the Lois and Richard Rosenthal Center for Contemporary Art—known as the Contemporary Arts Center—all that changed. It wasn't her first project, by any means. But with the opening of the building in downtown Cincinnati, the architectural world sat up and took notice as never before. Writing in *The New York Times*, architecture critic Herbert Muschamp described it as "the most important American building to be completed since the Cold War."

Even though she died in 2016, her reputation has continued to grow, particularly with the September 2019 opening of Beijing's Daxing airport. Critics ooh'd and aah'd its luminous, lighter-than-air feeling, with architecture writer Liz Stinson declaring it "a gleaming ode to modernity."

—David Lyman

JEFFERSON JAMES

Founder of Contemporary Dance Theater

Jefferson James has a life-long love for expressing herself through movement. When she was six, she told her parents she wanted to be a dancer. They listened, putting her in modern dance classes.

As a young girl, James visited New York and the acclaimed Graham Studios (so named for founder and modern dance icon Martha Graham) where she fell in love with Graham's groundbreaking dance technique. James broadened her horizons, taking everything from ballet at the Washington School of Ballet, to character and folk-dance classes, to tap, and even *bharatanatyam*, an Indian classical dance.

She went on to study at Julliard, where she met her now-husband, a musician. He took a job with the Cincinnati Symphony Orchestra (CSO), and the pair moved to the Queen City in 1964. James continued her studies at the University of Cincinnati's College-Conservatory of Music (CCM) at a time when modern dance in the Midwest was less common than on the East Coast. When her husband was drafted to serve in the Army Band during the Vietnam War, the couple moved to Virginia. The CSO held his job, and upon their return a few years later, James completed her degree at CCM. Modern dance had become, in the intervening years, its own field of study.

James saw abundant opportunity to solidify modern and contemporary dance's importance in Cincinnati. She choreographed works for other dancers, creating a program in 1970 called (appropriately) *Dance70*. This experiment led two years later to cre-

ating a full-fledged modern dance company called the Contemporary Dance Theater (CDT).

The new company spent several years rehearsing in various spaces and performing around Cincinnati, bringing dance to schools and community organizations. In 1985, CDT became part of the National Performance Network, which allows choreographers and companies to tour work around the country, including Cincinnati. CDT maintained its own company of dancers until 1995, when CDT shifted its focus to exclusively showcasing burgeoning new choreographic work via the Area Choreographer's Festival, now held annually at the Aronoff Center for the Arts.

James was awarded the 1998 Governor's Award for Arts Administration, as well as receiving choreographic fellowships from both the National Endowment for the Arts and the Ohio Arts Council. She believes contemporary dance brings humanity to the stage, and that seeing fellow human beings moving and presenting different ideas about the world through dance is essential, emotional, and profound. Her passion for contemporary dance remains as persistent and powerful as ever, as the Contemporary Dance Theater enters its 47th year of existence.

—Leyla Shokoohe

RUTH DENNIS SAWYER & MARY "MURPH" TAFT MAHLER

Founders of Ensemble Theatre Cincinnati

Two candles are lit in the lobby of Ensemble Theatre Cincinnati (ETC) for every performance. They represent the company's founding angels, Ruth Dennis Sawyer and Mary "Murph" Taft Mahler.

Sawyer and Mahler were leaders who were enormously talented and passionate about the art form they championed. A love of theater led Mary Mahler and her husband Ken, along with Ruth Sawyer and her husband John, to co-found ETC in 1986. But their passion didn't stop with purchasing and spending $3 million of their own money to transform the 1904 Greek revival building, a former bank, into the company's home on Vine Street in Over-the-Rhine. It continued with their recruitment of board members who would make it a success, and in rolling up their sleeves to paint sets and even perform as actors.

ETC launched in Memorial Hall for two seasons before opening in 1988 in the current building. They secured a contract with Actors Equity Association with the vision of creating a place to give work to local professionals, a concept that was unusual in the 1980s. ETC remains Cincinnati's second-largest professional theater.

The two women complemented each other. Sawyer bubbled over with enthusiasm, working nonstop to finish painting a set, often falling asleep in the theater where she'd be found, hard at work, the next morning. Mahler brought a soothing energy and calm faith that inspired the company to persevere even through the most difficult times.

Mahler, a Cincinnati native, was an accomplished singer who sang in the prestigious May Festival Cho-

rus and was a co-founder of the Musical Arts Center in O'Bryonville. At ETC, she served on the board and executive committee for more than 20 years. She performed in several ETC productions, notably her one-woman show *The Belle of Amherst* about her favorite poet, Emily Dickinson. Also an accomplished visual artist, Mahler studied at the Central Academy of Commercial Art in Cincinnati.

Sawyer was born in Kansas City, Missouri, where she became enamored with drama at the Barstow School for Girls. She continued acting at Briar Cliff College, cast in roles such as Julie Jordan in *Carousel*. It was there that she also began scenic design. She was active in directing, performing, and designing for community theater in Indian Hill when she was recruited to help with a fledgling company in Over-the-Rhine. For the first decade, Sawyer shared her talents as a set designer for many of ETC's mainstage productions, often donating her own furniture and props to use onstage.

Sawyer was an influential mentor to property master Shannon Lutz. "Ruth really taught me the definition of integrity and the selfless quality about working hard in support of others," Lutz said. "Many times, we deconstructed entire projects because she was not satisfied."

—Janelle Gelfand

D. LYNN MEYERS

Ensemble Theatre Cincinnati

D. Lynn Meyers returned to her hometown in 1995, charged with closing Ensemble Theatre Cincinnati (ETC), then a struggling company in a violent neighborhood infested by crime and drugs. She ended up staying.

She refused to abandon either the company or its Over-the-Rhine neighborhood as ETC clawed its way back from the brink.

Now in her 25th anniversary season (2019-20) as producing artistic director, Meyers has overseen an astonishing turn-around, crowned by a vibrant, $7 million renovation of the building and a 2019 Ohio Governor's Award for the Arts for Excellence in Arts Education. Her tenure and tenacity also earned Meyers Cincinnati's prestigious 2019 Sachs Fund Prize for outstanding accomplishments in the arts.

Through her vision and tenacity, Meyers became a catalyst in the revitalization of OTR. From the start, she enhanced the theater community by programming insightful plays with a social purpose.

"What Ensemble taught me was to try to let go of fear," Meyers said. "Everyone was so frightened—of Over-the-Rhine, frightened we were going to close, of doing new plays with a social conscience. There was something about releasing all of those fears and saying, 'The goal is so important that I'm not going to let fear stop me.' "

Her passion was, in part, personal. The descendant of German immigrants, her ancestors settled in the 19th century in Over-the-Rhine, just blocks from Ensemble Theatre. She grew up in Bridgetown, Ohio, and earned three degrees (BFA in theater, English, and education) from Thomas More University (then College). An opening at Cincinnati Playhouse in the Park evolved into a decade as she rose to associate artistic director and casting director.

From there, Meyers flourished as a freelance stage and casting director throughout the United States and Canada. She never dreamed of leading a professional theater company, in part because women artistic directors were rare at the time.

But Meyers was inspired by ETC co-founders Ruth Dennis Sawyer and Mary "Murph" Taft Mahler and their out-of-the-box idea of giving work to local professional artists, a goal that still makes her proud. After both Sawyer and Mahler had passed away, Meyers assumed the title of The Ruth Dennis Sawyer/Mary Taft Mahler Producing Artistic Director.

Early on, Meyers was at the forefront of American theater, mounting plays that addressed our humanity and gave voice to the disenfranchised, such as *Praying for Rain* on a topic of teen suicide. With ETC's mission of presenting new work, she has directed more than one hundred regional and world premieres. In the 2019-20 season, six of her seven plays are by women because they were, to her, the best scripts.

Her skills in casting are also evident in the more than 15 films that Meyers, as a member of the Casting Society of America, has cast for Cincinnati's growing film industry, including *Hillbilly Elegy*, *Carol*, *Miles Ahead*, and *Dark Waters*.

"The most important thing that I've given to the city is faith in the power of art to heal. I'd like to believe that people who've seen things like *Brownsville Song* and *Next to Normal* and *Fun Home*, that what they'll take away is not only the power to heal a neighborhood," she said. "It was letting my stubbornness turn into faith, and just committing to it. I hope that was a beacon for people to say, 'If Ensemble can do it, we can do it.'"

—Janelle Gelfand

CAROLYN WALLACE

Founder of It's Commonly Jazz

Carolyn Wallace is a woman who was ahead of her time. In 1985, long before lifestyle shopping centers became the norm, Wallace was general manager of Swifton Commons Mall in Bond Hill that was built in 1956.

As the first mall in Cincinnati, it was an open-air concept before that became popular, but had fallen on hard times in the mid-1980s. The mall was purchased by Ohio-based DeBartolo Corporation, then the world's largest shopping center developer. The DeBartolos hand-picked Wallace from Bond Hill Redevelopment Corporation to become the first (and only) African-American woman in the company.

Wallace credits the DeBartolos with giving her the freedom to help revitalize Swifton Commons and the genesis of It's Commonly Jazz.

It was a clever strategy. Every Thursday in July and August, Swifton's open-air commons hosted all types of music, including barbershop, R&B, jazz, and reggae. When the performance was over—bam! The lights went on, stores opened, and concert-goers became instant customers. Once inside, they were treated to curated art exhibits.

"I fell in love with jazz when I was 12. I used to listen to Oscar Treadwell (an American jazz radio presenter) while I did my homework." Some people might save for a car or buy new clothes with their first paychecks. Wallace bought her first jazz album.

Despite Wallace's strong programming efforts, tough economic times once again hit Swifton Commons in 1995. Wallace stayed on to help manage the nearly empty property until 1997 when it was purchased by Jordan Crossing Church. Soon she was called back to reinstate the jazz series. "People would show up on Thursdays expecting to hear music!"

After a year of respite from work, but keeping It's Commonly Jazz running, Wallace joined the Walnut Hills Redevelopment Foundation to lead its affordable home ownership program.

Always a food lover, home chef, and caterer to visiting artists, Wallace started making box lunches for meetings. She remembers vividly sitting at her desk in Walnut Hills on 9/11, listening to stories of people whose dreams had been tragically shattered. Carolyn's epiphany that day was to pursue her own dream of owning a full-time catering business. The Perfect Brew was born in 2001.

Wallace views her work as caterer and music promoter as two sides of a sustainable coin. Cooking healthy food became a way of expressing her values as a key ingredient of clients' events. Helping to sustain Cincinnati's local music industry fuels Wallace's passion. She says "I love the way that music (and food) crosses gender, race, economics—everything! There's such a wonderful diversity when people come together around a common bond."

In 2010, Wallace moved the venue for It's Commonly Jazz to the Seasongood Pavilion in Eden Park. "I just went to my favorite playground." Today the event is co-sponsored by the Cincinnati Parks Department and the Art Museum along with financial sponsors who make it possible to maintain free admission.

It's Commonly Jazz is about much more than the music. Recently Wallace shifted the lineup of artists to emphasize local musicians. "Now they don't have to leave town to get paid." She still brings in national artists, but makes sure there is a performance partnership with local artists. In yet another refinement, in 2019 all performers were invited to ask younger artists to play with them.

Join Wallace in Eden Park in August 2020 for the 35th anniversary celebration!!

—Kathy Merchant

LYDIA MORGAN

Founder of Juneteenth

Juneteenth founder Lydia Morgan's lifelong passion for learning and teaching entered a new phase when she decided to launch a Cincinnati chapter of an organization dedicated to celebrating the legal end of slavery in America on June 19, 1865.

Raised in Bolivia, North Carolina, in a farming family, Morgan went to Bennett College and majored in business before seeing a sign—literally—advertising a free master's degree in exchange for teaching. Morgan traveled to New Jersey for the program, meeting a diversity of people who would open her eyes to the many stories everyone has to share. She taught business in New Jersey before moving to Columbus, Ohio, to teach high school business and math, and then on to Xenia, Ohio, where she earned another degree in elementary education from Central State University. Morgan was eventually recruited by Sycamore Community Schools, teaching fifth grade for 25 years.

In 1987, Morgan accompanied her husband to Phoenix, Arizona, where he was attending a conference. While in Phoenix, Morgan was invited to attend Juneteenth—an event she'd never heard of. (In an interesting stroke of prescience, when she was nine, Morgan had asked her mother why Independence Day existed, celebrating the freedom of America from Great Britain, but no celebration of the freedom of black people from slavery.)

Her question was answered many years later. Morgan loved the celebration so much that she brought the concept and event back to Cincinnati, officially launching in 1988 at Drake Park in Kennedy Heights. Even with no advertising or marketing, some 1,500 people showed up. Attendance and interest have grown by leaps and bounds over the past 30+ years.

Today Juneteenth is a two-day celebration held in Eden Park that showcases the well- and lesser-known historical facts surrounding the end of slavery in the United States. An historical timeline illuminates events since 1865, including the Civil Rights movement, and Morgan expands the depth of the timeline every year by adding new facts and anecdotes. There's food, and performances from musicians—often Ohio greats (such as legendary funk band the Ohio Players)—and myriad product and information booths. The second day of the festival always celebrates Father's Day.

More than anything, Juneteenth celebrates what Morgan calls "the shared reality of being human." She hopes attendees will be able to evaluate their personal histories, learn more about the country's history, and share their experiences with others. Perhaps with an evolving understanding of what it means to be part of a diverse community with a common history, Cincinnati can become a better place.

—Leyla Shokoohe

JUNIOR LEAGUE OF CINCINNATI (1920)

The Association of Junior Leagues International was founded in 1901 by New Yorker Mary Harriman, the 19-year-old daughter of Union Pacific Railroad titan H.R. Harriman. In 1920, Junior League of Cincinnati (JLC) was among the first chapters.

Dissatisfied with the course of life befitting wealthy families, Miss Harriman eschewed debutante balls for college and social justice. She was inspired by women such as Jane Addams in Chicago and the Settlement House movement then taking root, and envisioned a way to "revolutionize the experience of young women being introduced to society." Today the organization is a worldwide network spanning four countries, more than 140,000 women, and over 290 chapters.

In 2020, the Junior League of Cincinnati ("the JLC") celebrates its 100th anniversary! A century ago, the founding members of the JLC felt the same call that inspired Mary Harriman. In Cincinnati, the inaugural project was the Babies Milk Fund, itself part of a national movement to reduce infant mortality and increase the health of surviving children. The JLC helped to establish four pediatric clinics across the city.

There isn't much that a cadre of nearly 1,000 women cannot not do! The JLC's mission is to be "committed to promoting voluntarism, developing the potential of women, and improving communities through the effective action and leadership of trained volunteers." In its first century, the JLC has incubated or accelerated over 140 programs that strengthen children including Fernside Center for Grieving Children, ProKids, and Kids Helping Kids, as well as its newest partnership with "Sweet Cheeks Diaper Bank."

The JLC's commitment to children has also fueled the vibrancy of arts and culture programs in Cincinnati. Four projects stand out as reflections of members' passion and power:

The Children's Theatre of Cincinnati (1919)
Cincinnati chapter member Helen Schuster-Martin started the Junior League Players, a theatrical troupe designed to educate and entertain children. For nearly 30 years, the JLC's members managed, acted in, and produced entertainment. In 1947, The Chil-

dren's Theatre incorporated as a separate entity, but continues a close relationship with the JLC.

Cincinnati Art Museum Docent Program (1960)
In partnership with Cincinnati Public Schools (CPS), the JLC designed an educational program for sixth graders to interpret the museum's permanent collection. Twenty-eight docents were trained to lead this program in CPS schools, and eventually at the Museum itself. In 1975, the Art Museum folded the program into its Education Department where the Docent Corps of over 100 volunteers continues to thrive.

Duke Energy Children's Museum—Cincinnati Museum Center (1994)
The concept for a children's museum in Cincinnati was driven by Darlene Kamine, past president of the JLC. After adopting the idea as a priority project, by 1994 the JLC had raised enough money to debut the Cincinnati Children's Museum at Longworth Hall. A major flood in 1997 forced the museum's evacuation. Its new home, then and now, is the Cincinnati Museum Center.

Cincinnati Fire Museum (1979)
Unknown to many is that Cincinnati was the first city in America to have a public fire department. Forty years ago, the Cincinnati Fire Museum was created to celebrate and preserve that important piece of history, and to educate children about fire safety. The JLC's past president, Nancy Kohnen Black, was the Fire Museum's first executive director.

—Kathy Merchant

Founding Board of Managers
Mrs. Lucien Wilson, Jr., President
Miss Mary Anderson, Vice President
Miss Eleanor Gholson, Second Vice-President
Miss Hebrietta Jones, Secretary
Miss Mary Waite, Treasurer

ANGELA WILLIAMSON

Founding General Manager of Kentucky Symphony Orchestra

Angela Williamson became the first General Manager of the Kentucky Symphony Orchestra (KSO) in 1996. Founder James R. Cassidy had served as music director and manager, operating on a wing and a prayer, for four years.

Initially called the Northern Kentucky Symphony, the fledgling orchestra grew to the point that it needed a manager. Williamson became the first (and only) person to hold that position.

The orchestra's name changed in 2001. The Williamson/Cassidy relationship changed as well—they married and have been working together ever since.

Williamson had never considered working for an arts organization until just a few years after obtaining her first two bachelor's degrees in music and accounting from Palm Beach Atlantic University (1992). And because she also went on to get masters' degrees in business administration and arts administration at the University of Cincinnati (UC), Williamson says, "I existed in two worlds for many years."

Pressured by faculty to pick a priority, Williamson declared music as an undergraduate major in order to get a music scholarship, which is what had initially afforded her the chance at her accounting degree. "My accounting advisor said, 'It's time for you to pick one major,'" she explains. "But my gut told me 'No!' "

The Kentucky Symphony Orchestra is fortunate to have attracted someone as a leader who is capable of holding and understanding both sides of the coin of an arts institution: carrying the financial load and empathizing with the artistic work involved in putting on each and every concert.

Being in her position for more than two decades has afforded the organization consistency of leadership with Williamson at the helm. "Consistency in leadership is vital, especially in smaller organizations. An arts organization's greatest assets are its people: artists, administrators, staff, board, volunteers, donors and audiences."

Her point bears repeating indeed: organizational leaders create a positive culture by setting priorities and cultivating community relationships. Though Williamson says she can't recall a time when she's ever felt that women were less capable than men, having strong women like UC professor and arts administration program co-director Karen Faaborg to learn from really helped Williamson articulate her ideas about arts governance and management.

She also cites other successful women "who have for decades raised the profile and continue to lead their respective Greater Cincinnati arts organizations: Patty Beggs, Victoria Morgan, Lynn Meyers, and Laurie Risch"—all of whom have helped shape Williamson's ideas around the trajectory of her own successful career as a woman in Cincinnati's arts.

In true artist/accountant form, Williamson says, "At the KSO, we find that balancing both realistic artistic and fiscal goals allows the entire team to move forward with consistency each season."

But Williamson says she looks to the precedent ArtsWave has set for Greater Cincinnati in terms of how performance art can elevate community "by putting a region on the map, deepening roots, bridging cultural divides, enlivening neighborhoods, and fueling creativity and learning."

Since the arts engender connectedness, it is no wonder that Williamson is both practical and passionate about her work. Her work and personal lives are intertwined in ways that clearly support her biological family as well as her symphony family. We could all hope to be cast in such a supportive role.

—Maria Seda-Reeder

KATHY WADE

Founder of Learning Through Art

In the spring of 1987, Kathy Wade was a Jazz diva in-the-making. Arguably, not even she knew what or who she would become: name-brand go-to Jazz singer, founder and CEO of Learning Through Art, Inc.

She was an ever-inventive entrepreneur, world traveler, mother, sage advisor to nascent black businesswomen, and sometimes melancholy widow.

Thirty-three years ago, she pushed through the glittery evening dresses of her friend's Victory Parkway apartment closet, stepping out for feedback. Wade was on her way to sing for showcase audiences at venerable New York Jazz clubs.

Fast forward, Wade is now a certified Diva-In-Repose and synonymous with the elegance and class Cincinnati's art world is accustomed to consuming.

She's worked humbly, hard and smart. And she's never forgotten her first published review in the *Cincinnati Post*. "Dale Stephens said (my voice was) 'a nuclear reactor where her vocal chords should be.' "

Among other firsts, she is the first black woman to receive a master's degree in art administration from the University of Cincinnati's College Conservatory of Music. Wade knew an advanced degree would propel her mission to sing the music she loves while using that music to sing the praises of self-confidence to generations of Cincinnati's school children.

Wade married her love of jazz music to her love of educating children and birthed a legacy. She started Learning Through Art, Inc. (LTA), in 1992 and *Books Alive! For Kids* (BAFK), its major program, followed in 1998.

The Emmy-nominated BAFK incorporates social/emotional learning techniques. "You can instantly change the trajectory of whoever is working with BAFK—kids, parents—because of the modality we use: touch, listening, sight."

LTA was quickly incorporated with nonprofit status during the heyday of rap music, inspiring Wade to start the *Black Anthology of Music*. "It's about the history of jazz and finishing what you started." It traces the historical timeline, interconnection and significance of Jazz, America's black classical music.

Students needed clarity, says Wade: "Kids thought turntable-scratching was an instrument."

Crown Jewels of Jazz is Wade's annual showcase of stalwart women singers she curates from America's girth of talent. It kicked off back in 1995 with headliner and hometown star Rosemary Clooney, since featuring Nancy Wilson, Diane Schur, Cleo Laine, and Shirley Horn.

All the ideas, programs, children's books and sweat equity emanate from Wade's spacious Bond Hill office/workspace. It is a bright respite; however, she doesn't rest on her many laurels there.

She is a 2019 recipient of a Haile Foundation People's Liberty Project Grant for "Loads of Love: Life Skills to Laundry." A laundromat morphed into a community center offering "a six-week, interactive workshop conducted between washing and drying cycles…Through guest speakers, hands-on activities and lessons, the project…taught simple and accessible life skills using social-emotional learning in 60 minutes."

Wade continues building upon the original LTA tenets so one day she can leave her business as an intact legacy. "It's working in a servant/service realm with an entrepreneurial spirit. There's nothing that says you can't sell what you do."

—Kathy Y. Wilson

CINCINNATI MUSEUM CENTER POST RENOVATION

MARIA LONGWORTH STORER *1849–1932*

Founder of Cincinnati May Festival

Maria Longworth Storer was a talented musician, versatile artist, and enterprising art patron. If that were not enough, her visions for a concert festival and an art manufacturing business were actualized in the 19th century, and both still exist today.

Storer was born into Cincinnati's affluent Longworth family who patronized artists and writers. Her creative potential was enhanced by her musically and artistically gifted mother who, it is believed, taught her to draw and play the piano. In the 1870 census, this twenty-one-year-old listed herself as an artist—quite a statement for a young married woman who was pregnant with her first child.

In the early 1870s, Storer gave piano concerts at home and on stage. She envisioned a multi-event choral and orchestra celebration. After an inspiring trip to Europe, she convinced noted orchestra conductor Theodore Thomas to direct the fledgling project and in 1873 convened a group of city boosters to organize and fund it. Storer and her then-husband, Col. George Nichols, provided the first $5,000 guarantee. Called the Cincinnati May Festival, the concert series was a tremendous artistic and financial success that brought national acclaim to the Queen City.

As a result, the organizers were encouraged to plan future festivals, build Music Hall, and create the College of Music. Storer supported the music series by translating German song lyrics, serving on committees, and hosting out-of-town guests for performances. Cincinnati May Festival is the second oldest music festival of its kind in the world (predated only by Britain's Three Choirs Festival founded in 1719).

Storer's appreciation for beauty inspired her to create decorative pottery. Her ceramic objects were quirky creations reflecting her highly individual aesthetic vision. In 1880, she established her own pottery called Rookwood Pottery after her father's estate. She wanted total control over every aspect of the process in this first woman-run manufacturing operation in the United States.

Storer was adept at employing the best local decorators, most of whom were trained artists. She positioned Rookwood in the precinct of fine art by selling her wares in upscale jewelry stores, loaning promotional items to art dealers, and donating special pieces to museums. She also hired William Watts Taylor who brought a business sense and made Rookwood profitable internationally. Rookwood would become the greatest art pottery business in America. It also promoted Cincinnati as an important center of the arts.

Over sixty years, Storer devoted much of her time, wealth and energy as an arts patron to the development of creative people, supporting their careers and reveling in their accomplishments. For example, she helped to establish Fedor Encke as a reputable portraitist. He painted Storer's father, Joseph Longworth, and her friend, President Theodore Roosevelt, to name a few. She also funded international study and training for gifted artists such as Artus Van Briggle, who later formed his own pottery in Colorado. And she paid the first year's salary for Frank Duveneck to come to Cincinnati to teach at the Art Academy in Eden Park.

A generous woman, Storer lent and gave many paintings, ceramics, textiles, and sculptures to the Cincinnati Art Museum. She also fostered Cincinnati history by giving family letters, scrapbooks, watercolors, and other ephemera to the Cincinnati Historical Society which is now maintained by the Cincinnati Museum Center.

Maria Longworth Storer was a creative genius, demonstrating how one woman's intelligence, drive and influence helped to transform Cincinnati into a cultural powerhouse.

—Constance Moore and Nancy Broermann

CATHERINE ROMA

Founder of MUSE Cincinnati Women's Choir

Catherine (Cathy) Roma is a transformative artistic director and choral activist driving change through music crossing gender, ethnic, religious, and socio-economic lines to open doors of understanding.

Roma's risk-taking spirit has paved the path for award-winning commissions and choirs focused on vocal empowerment and significant lyrics. As a musical pioneer with over a century of cumulative contributions, she has initiated and conducted four womens choirs, multiple prison choirs, and activist choral groups, along with commissioning new works that speak to the significance of women's lives. Her impact is felt far beyond the Queen City, showcasing that "(s)inging is a philosophy, a political statement, a social manifesto and joyful noise."

Musical family roots influenced Roma to play piano at an early age, but her incredible teachers helped her express feelings through music and influenced music as a vocation. Following her BA in Music, Roma began her first choir in 1971 at the Madison Community School. This experience and ties to the Philadelphia Quaker School led to switching her masters' degree focus in 1975 from piano to choral conducting.

Roma soon realized that she wanted to tell the story of American women. Her best friend Anne Dexter Gordon, an American colonial historian, pushed Roma to start a women's choir and featuring historical women's songs. This resulted in the *Anna Crusis Choir* delivering a women's history folk opera. The choir is still thriving in its 45th year. This endeavor coincided with her involvement in the "women's and gay & lesbian choral movements," both playing a critical role in defining who she is today.

While pursuing a Doctorate at the College-Conservatory of Music, Roma created MUSE, a preeminent women's choir dedicated to musical excellence and social justice currently in its 37th year. For nearly 30 years, she worked as minister of music at St. John Unitarian Universalist Church and partnered with Bishop Todd O'Neal to co-direct the *MLK King Chorale*. The *Chorale* performed at the opening of the National Underground Railroad Freedom Center in 2004.

Roma understands that music crosses boundaries and open minds. As *World House Choir* director, she leads a 100-voice community peace and justice organization. While working as a professor, she was part of the Wilmington College Prison Program, an ideal teaching situation where people are hungry to learn; she continues to direct three Ohio prison choirs today. Her leadership of these organizations helped enable a successful World Choir Games-Cincinnati in 2012.

In a life filled with extraordinary accomplishments, Roma continues to find happiness in music, driving change, and with her life partner, Dorothy Smith. Women's stories still fuel her efforts today. The Roma Commission premiers in 2020 with 17 women's choirs performing "Lifting As We Climb" to celebrate the 100th anniversary of women's right to vote, and her men's prison choral group is preparing to perform *The Hamilton Project*. She breaks through barriers and opens new territory, embracing people as individuals and creating opportunities to be and do more.

Cathy Roma is a musical force for change in a world that desperately needs it.

—Christi Geary

ELIZABETH WEICHER PIERCE

Cincinnati Museum Center

On a rainy summer morning, Elizabeth Pierce knows the rotunda of Cincinnati Museum Center will be filled with visitors.

She knows because, as the Museum Center's president and CEO, she's worked hard to build membership and increase admission income. She's also a mother who brings her own sons here; she knows what this place means to Cincinnati families.

She came to Cincinnati in 1999 with a bachelor of arts in history from Miami University and a masters degree in museum studies from George Washington University. Previously she'd served as director of development at Chicago Children's Museum. Pierce began working with the Cincinnati Museum Center twenty years ago as a communications consultant, then joined the staff as vice president for marketing and communications in 2007.

In 2015, Pierce took the helm of the Museum Center and led the organization through the recent $250 million restoration of the 1933 Union Terminal building. Her deep understanding of the needs of the iconic structure helped her build the case for the Union Terminal sales tax campaign, which passed with the support of 62 percent of Hamilton County voters.

Working with an army of architects, engineers, preservationists, consultants, volunteers, staff, and community leaders who were behind the massive project was exciting. Pierce says "everyone was jazzed because they all wanted to save the building." That enthusiasm was a lifeline during setbacks, such as the discovery that steel beams above the Children's Museum were more damaged than anticipated and had to be replaced. That meant more expense, closing the popular museum for months, re-deploying staff, and figuring out how to keep everything on track.

"We've got a phenomenal team," she says. "They rallied around all of this."

FRANCIE HILTZ

Cincinnati Museum Center

Francie Schott Hiltz knew Cincinnati Union Terminal long before it became Cincinnati Museum Center.

As a child, she was awed by the bustling station when her father, Milton Schott, returned from trips to see his brothers, Harold and Joe, in Cleveland. But her deeper connection began when she joined the Museum Center's board of trustees during the long, exacting process of determining what it would take to fix the tremendous structural problems of the Art Deco jewel. And as board chair during renovation, her leadership was a steady hand in the ups and downs of preserving this Cincinnati treasure.

She frequently does her community work behind the scenes, but in the thick of the Save Our Icons campaign to build support for a tax levy for the restoration of both Music Hall and the Museum Center at Union Terminal, Francie spoke to community groups and addressed the Hamilton County Commissioners. She claims to be a shy person, not accustomed to public speaking and new to the complications of city-county politics. But, she says in her typically understated fashion, "I got used to it."

Many city institutions have benefited from the strength of her thoughtful, calm resolve. She has served as chair of the Cincinnati Symphony Orchestra, on the executive committee of the Cincinnati Zoo and Botanical Garden, and a trustee of the Cincinnati Museum Center Foundation, among others. She and her husband, Tom, are trustees of the Harold C. Schott Foundation, which has given financial support to churches, hospitals, arts, and educational organizations.

The reason is simple, she says. "I love all of these places. What would this city be without them?"
—Linda Vaccariello

PATRICIA K. BEGGS

Cincinnati Opera

It's difficult to remember what the Cincinnati Opera was like before Patricia (Patty) Beggs became the company's marketing director in 1984. She wasn't specifically charged with re-branding the company.

But as an Opera subscriber and volunteer, she knew it needed a more up-to-date profile.

Previously, she had worked with a pair of large regional banks, Central Trust Company and Provident Bank. There she learned how very essential it was to not only be perceived as a modern company, but also to be one that focused on the experience of its customers.

Why couldn't Cincinnati Opera have the same sort of relationship with its patrons?

Growing up in suburban Dayton, Beggs' musical taste didn't run much deeper than what she and her friends listened to on Top 40 radio. That changed when she attended opera and symphony as a student in Boston in the early 1970s. Beggs was particularly inspired by the work of opera impresario Sarah Caldwell, the founder and wildly innovative leader of the Opera Company of Boston.

Later, upon moving to Cincinnati and continuing graduate business studies, Beggs stumbled upon a gem of an elective class taught by music professor Dr. Simon Anderson. It was Dr. Anderson, and his enormously popular music appreciation class at the University of Cincinnati College-Conservatory of Music, who cemented her love of opera. From there, Beggs' career shifted from bank marketing to the arts.

Beggs joined Cincinnati Opera already convinced that opera had the power to touch people emotionally, and in the process change hearts and minds. She was determined that her opera company would recreate the relevance, accessibility, and just plain fun of attending a live musical performance.

"We agreed that if we didn't talk about opera in a different way, the fate of the company—the entire art form—wasn't very good," Beggs told *Movers*

and Makers magazine in 2019. "Cincinnati Opera was within a couple hundred thousand dollars of folding every year." Attendance was dismal, and the Opera was operating on a very thin margin.

Beggs' promotional campaigns were regarded by some as saucy and racy. But they presented opera as a contemporary art, as something that could hold its own against film and theater and other popular entertainments. The approach was immediately successful, with attendance jumping 20 percent during Beggs' first season.

In 1991, she was promoted to assistant managing director, and took on the top administrative position in 1997. Following the 2004 season, she became general director and CEO.

During her tenure, the company has morphed from a traditional and relatively stodgy institution into one that is known for its innovation in developing new operas with socially relevant themes, and presenting world premieres as well as rousing productions of the standards.

Most important, she has created an organization that has led the way in its commitment to diversity and inclusion. It is both fiscally sound and a vital component of Cincinnati's cultural fabric. Like the city's other arts anchors, Cincinnati Opera is now as committed to carving out the future of its art form as it is reflecting on its past.

That is, in large part, thanks to the leadership of Patty Beggs.

In March of 2019, Beggs announced that she plans to retire in 2020, at the end of her own 35th anniversary with the company and the Cincinnati Opera's 100th anniversary season.

—David Lyman

TRACY WILSON

Cincinnati Opera

No one knew what to expect the first time Tracy Wilson took opera to church. She'd been lobbying Cincinnati Opera for a couple of years before she got the go-ahead to try something new in 2006.

As the Opera's director of community relations, she was determined to stretch the company's reach from Music Hall to the city's many neighborhoods.

There was skepticism, she recalls. "The opera people thought the church people would show up and the church people thought the opera people would."

As she stood in the sanctuary at Allen Temple AME, something else entirely unfolded. People started showing up by the hundreds—opera, gospel, and jazz lovers as well as people who were just curious about the combined music experience. About 1,500 people all-told, enough to require setting up extra speakers and chairs so all could hear.

Wilson reveled in the experience. "It was great seeing people from various backgrounds sitting shoulder-to-shoulder, listening to world renowned opera singers, a dynamic church choir, and powerhouse jazz musicians, all in the same place." And it continues to grow. In 2019, more than 4,000 people attended.

Opera Goes to Church is just one marker of the impact Tracy's had on the Cincinnati Opera in her 35 years with the company. Hers is an arc of legacy that mirrors that of Patty Beggs, the Opera's general director & CEO. What started as a part-time job selling tickets grew into a career—what Tracy calls a ministry—that has leveraged her innate exuberance and deep community connections.

"I grew up with three things. God, family, and community," she recalls. "It's a gift and a charge from Him to be a good steward and to do what He wants me to do and how He wants it."

Fulfilling that mission hasn't always been easy. Having grown up in richly diverse neighborhoods, the "high level of privilege and elitism" around grand opera in the 1980s was something new for her. Tracy was a trailblazer, the first and only person of color on the opera team.

Wilson felt compelled to speak up for people who weren't in the room. "It blew my mind that neighborhood kids could walk past Music Hall and have no idea what was inside."

So she welcomed them in through the Community Open Dress Rehearsal, which celebrates its 30th year in 2020. On this night, hundreds of kids are the VIPs at Music Hall after pre-opera festivities in Washington Park. *Cinderella* is on the stage? There are free shoes to take home. *The Barber of Seville*? Try on a free haircut. For a production of *Romeo & Juliet*, welcome to spoken word and song about romance, tragedy, and trauma performed by teens.

As the Cincinnati Opera has evolved into an organization that embraces and celebrates inclusion, Tracy has also contributed to the artistic product, setting up community programs and workshops for commissioned works like *Margaret Garner* and conducting interviews with exonerees for *Blind Injustice*.

She is also an artist herself, leading The Firelytes Steel Drum Band, and she is a voracious recorder of the world around her, capturing history though the lenses of still and video cameras.

—Mary Stagaman

CAST OF "CINCINNATI KING," 2018 WORLD PREMIERE, CINCINNATI PLAYHOUSE IN THE PARK.

LOIS ROSENTHAL *1939–2014*

Cincinnati Playhouse in the Park

Lois Rosenthal was a philanthropist with such a wide range of interests that it was difficult to step into the community and *not* see evidence of her generosity, though her patronage often extended well beyond Cincinnati.

She was tireless in her desire to be of service to the city where she was born and raised. Rosenthal was not one of those philanthropists content to write a check and go on her way. She shared her ideas, philosophy, and opinions—some quite strong—as well.

Depending on your area of interest, you might have a completely different understanding of her good deeds. For some, she was the person who, along with her husband Richard, championed and underwrote the production of new plays at the Playhouse in the Park. And because of her devotion to education, not all of those plays were for adult audiences. She also supported the Rosenthal Next Generation Theatre Series, which introduced more than 76,000 students and their parents to live performances by storytellers, musicians and dancers.

To others, she was responsible—again, with her husband—for bringing Zaha Hadid onboard as the architect of the new Contemporary Arts Center. Or for developing the Rosenthal Fresh Food Initiative at the Freestore Foodbank. Or establishing the Ohio Innocence Project. Or for founding Uptown Arts, a tuition-free arts education center located in the middle of one of the city's poorest neighborhoods.

She was central to so many programs and projects, it sometimes felt that she was in a rush to accomplish more. The Rosenthals underwrote free admission at the Cincinnati Art Museum, then followed it up by creating the education center there. They created the Rosy Reader program to distribute free books to inner-city schools. They underwrote new play production at the Ensemble Theatre Cin-

cinnati and helped launch an internship program for high school students at the Cincinnati Zoo. And they founded Uptown Arts in Over-the-Rhine to provide free dance classes for inner-city children.

Indeed, she was so prolific with her community philanthropy that many people weren't aware of how very creative she was with her own projects. In 1975, she wrote Living better in *Cincinnati: A Guerrilla Guide to Getting the Most for Your Money*, a regional bestseller that introduced readers to lesser-known stores, restaurants, parks, artists, and much more. It was in many ways a precursor to so many of her other activities celebrating the abundant opportunities that the region offers. In turn, that led to a weekly column in the *Cincinnati Enquirer*.

An especially gratifying project arose in 1989, when she and her husband resurrected a dormant literary magazine named *Story*. She was the editor, while Dick was the publisher. For a decade, until the sale of the family's F&W Publications, the quarterly publication published new fiction by writers, both established and up-and-coming. In time, it reached a circulation of 40,000, remarkable for such a serious-minded literary journal. It was, however, typical of the effort and passion with which Rosenthal approached everything she did.

Dick Rosenthal described it best in an obituary published by the *Cincinnati Enquirer*. "Any time you cracked the door for Lois, get out of the way," he said, "because she would go flying through and make all kinds of things happen."

—David Lyman

ELLEN
VAN DER HORST

Cincinnati Playhouse in the Park

For Ellen van der Horst, it all began with a toy piano. "My grandmother heard me play, concluded I had talent, and when I was nine bought me a Wurlitzer spinet. That really started my lifelong love of the arts."

A native of Philadelphia, van der Horst was raised on Broadway music, played the piano "pretty well," and did a "little bit" of acting in high school and college. "I had the dubious distinction of playing the title role in (Kurt Vonnegut's) *Happy Birthday, Wanda June* at the University of Pennsylvania," she said. "Playing a little kid was not a great way to kick off my college social life."

Van der Horst has turned her love of the arts into decades of fruitful action, guiding and strengthening several Cincinnati arts groups while pursuing an extraordinary business career.

After graduating from the prestigious Wharton School, she came to Cincinnati to work for Procter & Gamble in 1978. Five years later, she moved to PNC Bank, where she ultimately became executive vice president and chief marketing officer for retail banking.

In an early executive role at PNC, van der Horst was tapped to join the Cincinnati Opera board. "I had never been to an opera, but I thought it couldn't be all that different from a Broadway musical—well maybe a few surcaps…" She grew to love the art form, and at the age of 36, became the first female chair of the Cincinnati Opera board.

And that was only the beginning. She served for many years on the Fine Arts Fund board, where she helped lead its allocations process and was a key player in the transition to a new, more inclusive vision of the arts conveyed in the organization's new name, ArtsWave. For these efforts and more, van der Horst was named a Life Trustee.

After 22 years in banking, van der Horst embarked on a second act in 2006 when she was tapped by the Cincinnati USA Regional Chamber to become its first female president and CEO. She took the job with the goal of reversing the region's brain drain, creating opportunities to attract and retain young workers. That dovetailed nicely with her aim to strengthen and expand audiences for the arts. "A vibrant arts and culture scene draws young talent— and to businesses chasing that young talent," she said. And it's good for the community.

Her retirement from the Chamber in 2014 made time for van der Horst to take another deep-dive into the arts. Having served previously on the board of Cincinnati Playhouse in the Park, she was invited to rejoin the leadership of the Tony-award-winning theater. Her response was "only if I can play a meaningful role." It was an easy decision for van der Horst to say yes, but be careful what you wish for … she is stepping up to chair the Playhouse board as it transforms its facility in Eden Park. "Our exceptional regional theater deserves a home that is equal to the quality of its work."

"I have had the honor to be involved in so many things that make Cincinnati a better place," she said. "I have even more time now to enjoy this city, to make a difference, and that's what I intend to do." Despite her history of being a trailblazer for women in business and the arts, her most significant accomplishments may lie ahead. Watch for the new Rouse Theatre scheduled to open in late 2022.

—Ray Cooklis

KJ SANCHEZ

Cincinnati Playhouse in the Park

Director and playwright KJ Sanchez lives by the principle of following the pathways of her interests. Born in New Mexico, the youngest of 12 children, Sanchez took a school field trip to New York City and knew that's where she wanted to be.

After graduating from the University of California at San Diego, she was invited by theater director Ann Bogart to join SITI Company—an international theater company specializing in new works and training young artists—and moved to New York. Sanchez traveled the world performing, subsidizing her theater career with voice acting for cartoons, including *Dora the Explorer.*

A self-described problem solver, Sanchez soon realized that her true heart lay in writing and directing. As an independent playwright, she has written and directed several plays in the genre of docudrama. With New York actress and playwright Emily Ackerman, she co-authored *ReEntry* based on the experiences of Marines returning from Iraq and Afghanistan and their active-duty relationships with civilians in those countries. The work was critically acclaimed by theaters across the country and has been performed more than 50 times at various military hospitals and bases in the U.S. and abroad.

Another humanistic play, *X's and O's*, is about the brain trauma suffered by NFL star Junior Seau, who took his own life in 2012. Sanchez reached for deep realism in the play by conducting numerous interviews with other football players who had experienced the same on-field injuries as Seau.

In 2010, Sanchez founded American Records: A Theater Company. As CEO, she pursues the company's mission "To make theater that chronicles our time (and create) work that serves as a bridge between people."

Sanchez's interests had taken her to documentary plays, which is, fittingly, how she came to Cincinnati. Playhouse in the Park's artistic director Blake Robison had produced *ReEntry* in Maryland at the Round House Theatre. When he joined Playhouse, Robison hired Sanchez as an associate artist. She has directed several plays for the company, including *Jane Eyre*, *Sherlock Holmes*, and *Venus in Fur*. In 2018, through her company American Records, Sanchez created and directed *Cincinnati King*. Based on the life of groundbreaking music pioneer Syd Nathan, the play examines the iconic King Records studio and its Cincinnati roots.

In recent years, Sanchez has received a number of prestigious awards including a Fox Foundation Resident Actor Fellowship; invitation to deliver the 2013 Douglass Wallop Lecture in Theater & Performance; and in 2014 for her play *X's and O's*, the Rella Lossy Award which is given to professionally oriented theater organizations.

Sanchez's approach to her work is defined by careful examination and sturdy determination. She is currently the head of the MFA directing program and an associate professor at the University of Texas at Austin, helping students discover their own pathways of interests.

—Leyla Shokoohe

MARNI PENNING

Founder of Cincinnati Shakespeare Company

Marni Penning, a native of Arlington, Virginia, was a Cincinnati theater pioneer. She graduated in 1992 from James Madison University and worked as an actor for the Shenandoah Shakespeare Express.

She traveled and performed in the U.S. and Great Britain while simultaneously seeking a city that might embrace a classic theater. She and her colleagues settled on Cincinnati and established Fahrenheit Theatre Company, committed to classics and new works.

Given the city's enthusiasm for other classic arts—symphony, ballet, theater, and visual art—the audience's greatest appetite was for works by Shakespeare and other renowned British, American and European playwrights. Penning was the talented actress around whom many productions revolved as Fahrenheit evolved into the Cincinnati Shakespeare Festival in 1997. (It became Cincinnati Shakespeare Company in 2006.) She was known for her ability to render Shakespearean blank verse in a remarkably conversational manner.

But Penning was more than an actress. She had marketing experience and graphic design talent, so she became the company's de facto marketing director. She designed CSF's first logo, a caricature of Shakespeare she drew on a napkin. She created posters, brochures and advertisements. She landed the company's first season sponsor and connected with local media to keep the fledgling company in the public eye. She organized actors to distribute posters for windows at local businesses. And she mentored many of the young actors (almost all in their 20s at first), making group meals and providing moral support.

Penning was passionate about attracting Cincinnatians to their own classical theater, enlivened by exciting young actors who loved Shakespeare. Support came out of the woodwork and built a strong foundation for the company's future success—now in its 27th season. "We were in the right place at the right time," she says, "and too young to think we could possibly fail. So it worked."

Nancy Helwig was a faithful volunteer with the theater company in its early days. "Anything that needed to be done, Marni did: photography, design, locating venues and, of course, acting." Penning got people to do all sorts of things, including recruiting Helwig's husband Bob to repair seats when the company moved into a former movie theater.

Penning excelled at connecting with other theaters and arts organizations, planting the seeds for today's flourishing theater scene where actors from CincyShakes perform frequently at Know Theatre, Ensemble Theatre Cincinnati, and Cincinnati Playhouse in the Park.

Once she became an Equity professional in 2000, Penning moved on to acting in New York City. She's performed across the country and in movies and television series. Now settled in Washington, D.C., she's married to John Coleman, who's not from the world of theater. Their son was born in 2012. She acts regularly at venues including Washington's Wooly Mammoth Theatre Company, Round House Theatre, Shakespeare Theatre Company, and Studio Theatre, as well as Shakespeare companies in Orlando, Atlanta, and Pennsylvania. She also narrates audio books.

Penning is a class act, an enthusiastic arts promoter, and was a super catalyst for Cincinnati's burgeoning arts community.

—Rick Pender

HELEN LOUISE "NELLIE" HERRON TAFT *1861–1943*

Founder of Cincinnati Symphony Orchestra

Nellie Herron Taft's ambition and adventurous spirit drove her to many outstanding achievements—on her own and as the wife of William Howard Taft, who served as governor of the Philippines, U.S. President, and Chief Justice of the U.S. Supreme Court.

At the age of 16, Taft had already decided she would marry a man who would become president. This desire was prompted by a family visit to the White House in 1877 at the invitation of President Rutherford B. Hayes, who was a former law-partner and long-time friend of her father, John Herron.

She was married to William H. Taft in 1886. Her biographer, Carl Sferrazza Anthony says "…in Will Taft she had finally found exactly what she had always described as her 'ideal'—a traditional marriage to an untraditional husband" who would see her as an intellectual equal. Anthony asserts it was Nellie's ambition that made Will Taft president: "Although everyone knew that Will's life-long ambition was to be on the Supreme Court, hers was for him to be president—and he deferred to her."

In 1893, restless from child-rearing and wifely duties, she joined with other socially prominent women to organize the Ladies Musical Club. This led to the founding of the Cincinnati Symphony Orchestra in 1895, with Taft as its first president. She was a hands-on manager who fought fiercely to hire Frank Van der Stucken as the Symphony's first conductor.

When her husband agreed to head the American civil government in the Philippines as Governor-General in 1900, Taft fully embraced this mission. She and the children moved to Manila where she entertained avidly and worked to reassure the local people by learning the language, wearing native costume, and inviting Filipinos to social events. Further travel with her husband, who became Secretary of War in 1904, broadened her knowledge of world politics and enriched her social network.

When her husband became president in 1909, Taft was an unconventional First Lady who broke precedent with many firsts. She was the first First Lady to ride with her husband after the Inauguration from the Capitol to the White House. She was the first First Lady to publish her memoirs, to own and drive a car, to support women's suffrage, to smoke cigarettes, and to successfully lobby for safety standards in federal workplaces. She was the first First Lady to attend a presidential nominating convention (1912), to donate her Inaugural gown to the Smithsonian Institution (1912), and to be buried in Arlington National Cemetery (1943).

Perhaps her most widely appreciated achievement was instigating the planting of cherry trees in the nation's capital in her first weeks as First Lady. Thanks to Taft, viewing the cherry blossoms has been a beloved spring ritual for over a century.

—Beth Sullebarger

Cincinnati Orchestra Association Company Founding Board of Directors May 1894

Helen "Nellie" Herron Taft, president
Laura McDonald Stallo, first vice president
Louise Nettleton Anderson, second vice president
Sarah "Sallie" Howard Woolley, secretary
Edith Perry Forchheimer, corresponding secretary
Isabel Jelke, treasurer
Helen Fletcher Huntington Chatfield
Virginia Ramsey Wright
Helen Fechheimer Stix
Helen Verhage Poland
Anna "Annie" Sinton Taft
Emma Roedter
Mary C. Stanwood Wilby
Babette "Bettie" Robertson Fleischmann Holmes
Henriette Schneider Billing

MARY JUDGE

Cincinnati Symphony Orchestra

Mary Judge made history when she became the United States' first full-time female orchestra librarian in 1975. Being an orchestra librarian is what she's always wanted to do, ever since she attended a Chicago Symphony Orchestra concert with her father in the 1950s.

They sat in the last row of the upper-most balcony. At the end of the concert, she was fascinated by the man who came onto the stage to gather all of the music. Judge's father took her to meet the music-gatherer, and the rest was history. She went to school the next day with a proposition for the music teacher: she would receive free violin lessons in exchange for acting as the school's orchestra librarian. She had a deal.

In high school, Judge bargained for composition and piano lessons, too. She attended Indiana University, acting as the orchestra librarian there for the school's two orchestras, and graduated with a degree in composition. Judge began working for the Cincinnati Symphony Orchestra (CSO) in 1975, celebrating her 45th season in 2019–20.

Orchestra librarians are considered members of the orchestra, as important as a principal cellist or oboist. They need to be able to read and transpose music, source and order music from publishers, time every piece, and prepare the music for any time the orchestra plays. Often conductors will give Judge a score with a multitude of handwritten notes, which she (and a small team of assistants) must then notate on each copy of music. Nothing goes on stage without a librarian's hands touching it first. Judge's favorite part of her job is being part of a 100 plus-piece puzzle.

For Judge, that joy came full circle when her own compositions were performed by the CSO. *Fanfare for a New Decade* was performed in the 1984–1985, 1985–1986, and 1989–1990 seasons. *Fanfare for a Celebration* was commissioned as part of the orchestra's centennial season, performed by the Orchestra during the 1995–1996 season under CSO's then-conductor Jesus Lopez-Cobos. It was also performed the following season under Cincinnati Pops conductor John Morris Russell.

During her tenure at the CSO, Judge has trained and sent numerous orchestra librarians out into the field, a distinction of which she is very proud. In addition to her work with the CSO, she is heavily involved in playing handbells for the Northminster Presbyterian Church in Finneytown and played in another local group for six years. She was also a founder of the Major Orchestra Librarians Association (MOLA,) a national convening organization for orchestra librarians.

The mother of three, including twins delivered when she was 50, Judge relishes her role as mom. Perhaps not coincidentally, she is an avid collector of vintage children's books (more than 5,000). She is also passionate about childhood literacy and led the charge for Cincinnati Public Schools to have a teacher specializing in dyslexia placed in every school.

—Leyla Shokoohe

SUE FRIEDLANDER

Cincinnati Symphony Orchestra

Even at age 15, Sue Friedlander (she was Sue Steinharter then) was an advocate for the Cincinnati Symphony Orchestra (CSO). Her 16-year-old boyfriend, Bill Friedlander, at Walnut Hills High School had never been to a concert.

She invited him and wrote afterwards in her scrapbook, "I finally got him to go to the symphony with me, and you know what? It didn't hurt him a bit!"

They married in 1955; Bill was in the army and Sue finished her bachelor of arts degree at Mount Holyoke College in Massachusetts. After his discharge, Bill attended Harvard Business School. Once he finished there, they returned to Cincinnati, living in Wyoming, where Sue worked as an assistant school librarian (1972–1985) and volunteered for several social service organizations.

Bill became a Cincinnati Symphony Orchestra board member. Sue served on the city's Arts Allocation Committee making small grants to artists and organizations. She joined the board of the Fine Arts Fund (now ArtsWave) and was asked to monitor the Cincinnati Ballet's finances in the late 1980s. Several arts organizations were struggling, but oversight by Sue and other volunteers helped restore order. "We worked ourselves out of a job just by meeting quarterly and overseeing (their work)," she says modestly.

Sue also served on the Fine Arts Fund's Projects Pool panel, providing small one-time grants to worthy organizations. That led to her participation on the Fund's Smaller Arts Review Committee, which made sweeping recommendations about funding for small and mid-sized organizations, significantly strengthening many of them.

In 1996 Sue and Bill, who at that time chaired the money management firm Bartlett & Co., were invited to a conversation about the CSO. They anticipated an ask for a gift, but they were actually recruited to co-chair the orchestra's Second Century endowment campaign. Bill was hesitant, but Sue urged him to give it more thought. Over dinner he said, "I think we can do it." Sue was excited, but laughingly wondered, "Will the marriage survive this? But it was good! It worked."

Indeed it did. They suggested the $15 million goal was too small and increased it twice. By the time the drive concluded, with Sue and Bill's leadership, $35.4 million was raised, doubling the orchestra's endowment. Ann Santen, retired general manager of WGUC-FM and a current CSO board member said, "Through Sue and Bill's extraordinary fundraising efforts and their own generosity they surpassed the goal and guaranteed the financial stability of our orchestra."

The Friedlanders were honored with the Post-Corbett Lifetime Achievement Award in 1997 and the Greater Cincinnati Foundation's 2009 Jacob E. Davis Volunteer Leadership Award. Sue was a 1998 *Enquirer* Woman of the Year.

When Bill passed away in 2014, Sue continued to endow the Ballet's artistic director position, a gesture they had both supported. She also chaired a campaign to support the 2017 expansion of Ensemble Theatre Cincinnati and funded the residency of the renowned Ariel Quartet at the College-Conservatory of Music.

Sue Friedlander's passion for the arts remains strong. "The arts are invaluable to our city," she says. "It's been proven that the arts, especially music, play an essential role in education."

—Rick Pender

DEBORAH EMONT SCOTT

Taft Museum of Art

Deborah Emont Scott has always known what she wanted to accomplish in life, but some of those accomplishments were helped into fruition by a bit of serendipity as well as determination. Scott believes leadership can't be taught.

However, it can be improved through mentorship—like the kind she has received in her career.

Growing up in Passaic, New Jersey, less than 20 miles from New York City, she knew she wanted to move to the Big Apple. And so she did, right after graduating from Rutgers University with a degree in English. She wanted to study art history in graduate school, but wanted to work first. And so she did, getting a job at an art gallery on Madison Avenue.

Two years later, Scott got a full ride to Oberlin College to pursue that planned graduate degree in art history. In a twist of fate that would set the stage for working in Cincinnati, her master's thesis was focused on John Henry Twachtman, a Cincinnati artist, and on Rookwood Pottery, a Cincinnati legacy company.

Scott's career moved forward quickly at Oberlin's Allen Memorial Art Museum, first as a curatorial assistant and then as an assistant curator. While there, Scott had a summer internship in the education department at the St. Louis Art Museum where she met Jay Gates, who become director of the Memphis Brooks Museum of Art. He offered her a job as curator there, and so she went.

The serendipity story soon snowballed. While working in Memphis, Scott met her now-husband, Andy. In Boston. At Logan International Airport. He'd come to meet her and a friend. She took a long look at him and knew straightaway that they would marry. Scott's connection with Jay Gates came back into play when he called her about an open position as the curator of modern and contemporary art at the Nelson-Atkins Museum of Art in Kansas City. (Andy

Scott was working in Kansas City.) She applied and got the job.

Scott spent 25 years in Kansas City, being promoted from associate to chief curator at the Nelson-Atkins Museum while raising her two daughters. She left that position in 2008, and so was open to a new opportunity when a friend told her about the available director position at the Taft Museum of Art in Cincinnati. Coincidentally, she had attempted to visit the museum back in her Oberlin days, but it was closed that day. In 2009, when she was invited to take on the role of Louise Taft Semple President/CEO— only the sixth director in 77 years—an opportunity to visit the Taft Museum of Art would be hers every day.

At the Taft Museum of Art, Scott is responsible for setting the agenda for the museum, overseeing fundraising, assessing potential exhibitions, and selecting gifts of artwork. The Taft Museum is one of the finest historic house museums in the country. Originally built in 1820 for Martin Baum, its second owner was Nicholas Longworth, who commissioned the impressive Duncanson murals that still grace the home today. Third owners Anna Sinton and Charles Phelps Taft assembled a permanent collection of 690 pieces of art from 1902–1927, and bequeathed both the house and the collection to the people of Cincinnati in 1927. Today's modern Sinton Gallery is dedicated to featuring exhibitions by living artists.

Under Scott's leadership, the beautifully tended Taft house will celebrate its bicentennial in 2020.

—Leyla Shokoohe

VERNITA HENDERSON *1948–2016*

Taft Museum of Art

If you attended live jazz shows at any of Cincinnati's music venues throughout the 2000s, you more than likely crossed paths with Vernita Henderson—usually adorned in a chunky piece of her own attention-grabbing jewelry designs.

Henderson was a jazz connoisseur who used her influence as chair of the Duncanson Artist-in-Residence Program at the Taft Museum of Art to accent events with the music she loved whenever possible.

"Working with her was always a joy," said jazz pianist/composer William Menefield, a School for Creative and Performing Arts graduate who became the youngest recipient of the Duncanson residency in 2002. "She was heavily involved in programming at the Taft, so she would bring me on for accompaniment or for combos at events there. She believed in me."

Of course, Menefield wasn't the only person whose talent Henderson believed in and nurtured. Under her leadership, the residency program has honored the likes of painter Brian Joiner, authors Sharon Draper and Nikki Giovanni, jazz vocalists Kathy Wade and Carla Cook, and dancer Stafford C. Berry, Jr.

The Duncanson Artist-in-Residence Program was established in 1986 to honor the achievements of contemporary African-American artists working in a variety of disciplines. It is an offshoot of the Robert S. Duncanson Society, which celebrates the relationship between African-American painter Robert S. Duncanson and his patron, Nicholas Longworth, who commissioned Duncanson to paint landscape murals in the foyer of his home. Henderson's leadership of the residency program spanned three decades until her death in 2016.

"She was a dynamo who kept the committee focused and productive," said photographer Melvin Grier, who worked with Henderson helping to select artists through the residency's advisory committee, and who is also a past recipient of the award. "I

mostly remember her distinctive laugh and sense of fashion style."

An artist in her own right, Henderson was primarily known for creating intricate jewelry pieces made from colorful natural stones, a love she shared with others through her own personal style as well as through a lucrative jewelry making business.

Writer and communications consultant C. Denise Johnson remembers Henderson from her involvement with the Arts Consortium of Cincinnati, the city's biggest coalition of African-American artists. "Vernita always had a unique sense of style that reflected her appreciation of art," said Johnson, who with Henderson was in the first class of the Urban League of Greater Southwestern Ohio's African American Leadership Development program. "She always struck me as being comfortable in her skin."

Deborah Emont Scott, the director of the Taft, has a memory of Vernita that she says she will always cherish. They sat together in the audience at the National Underground Railroad Freedom Center when DAIR artist Adrianne Danrich performed her *An Evening in the Harlem Renaissance* dance piece. Scott thought the performance was beautiful and moving, but when she looked over at Henderson, she had tears running down her face.

"Vernita felt things deeply," Scott said. "She was focused, she was intense, and I knew that whatever she said or did was not said or done lightly. The Taft Museum of Art is a better organization because of Vernita Henderson."

—Aiesha Little

SALLIE ROBINSON WADSWORTH *1936–2017*

Taft Museum of Art

Sallie Robinson Wadsworth saw the arts as a necessity, not a luxury. In 2019, Sallie and her husband, Randolph "Duck" Wadsworth, were recognized with the Ohio Governor's Award for the Arts for a lifetime spent supporting the arts across Greater Cincinnati.

Wadsworth was born in 1936 and attended Walnut Hills High School before earning her degree from Smith College. Although her degree was in English, she also had a head for numbers. She worked as an office manager and tax preparer for H&R Block for more than 20 years, and served as treasurer for the Taft Museum of Art.

Wadsworth's work at the Taft began in 1971 when she joined the first docent class. For four decades, she was a vital volunteer and supporter of the Museum. As a board member from 1985 to 2015, Sallie developed close working relationships with past and current curators and directors, including Lynne Ambrosini, Deputy Director and the Sallie Robinson Wadsworth Chief Curator at the Taft. Ambrosini remembers Sallie as soft-spoken and genteel, but also very shrewd, insightful, and a person who acted on her beliefs.

"Sallie didn't do anything that she didn't take seriously," Duck Wadsworth said.

A $5 million gift from Sallie, given after her death, established an endowment for the chief curator position, ensuring that self-organized exhibitions advancing scholarship will be a priority for the Taft. Sallie always aimed to elevate the museum to the next level, said Taft President and CEO Deborah Emont Scott. "She understood what the mission of the museum was and she wanted to help advance it….She wanted to allow us to dream and then turn those dreams into reality."

Over the decades, Wadsworth provided critical financial support to a variety of projects at the Taft.

She and her husband, for instance, were the lead supporters for the *Daubigny, Monet, Van Gogh: Impressions of Landscape* exhibition catalogue, research and symposium. The catalogue was especially important to her, Scott said, because that's the thing that lasts and shapes how people will view the art and artists.

In addition to the Taft, Sallie served on the boards of Cincinnati Playhouse in the Park, the Oxford Community Arts Center, the Ox-Act Community Theater, and a variety of other organizations. She led the Special Projects Pool of the Cincinnati Institute of Fine Arts (now ArtsWave), served as president of the Children's Theatre of Cincinnati, and was the first woman Chairman of the Board of McCullough-Hyde Memorial Hospital in Oxford.

She and her husband also were major supporters of the Cincinnati Symphony Orchestra—in 2014, the Wadsworths donated an undisclosed amount to help sustain the CSO as a 52-week orchestra— and many other arts organizations, including concert:nova.

Wadsworth once wrote in a letter to former Taft Museum Director Phillip Long that she found it "blush-making" to have her name attached to financial reports and often supported organizations anonymously. But if you love and enjoy the arts in Greater Cincinnati, you should know the name Sallie Robinson Wadsworth.

—Hillary Copsey

WOMAN'S ART CLUB (1892)

"The weather was clear and cool. The (Ohio) river was nine feet and falling. Business was fair at the wharf. Shillito's was advertising gifts for Christmas, and McCullough's, holly wreaths and trees.

Palatial side-wheel steamers were traveling east to Pittsburgh and south to New Orleans…(There were) forty-three breweries…" The *Cincinnati Enquirer's* Almanac for 1896 declared "the Cincinnati Art Museum (to be) the finest endowed institution of its kind on the continent and the Art School, in connection with it, the most perfect in its appointments."

Such was the state of Cincinnati in 1892 when nineteen women met in local artist Mary Spencer's studio on a chilly December day to sign the charter establishing The Woman's Art Club of Cincinnati, one of the first of its kind in the United States. Two years earlier, a group of 13 members of an informal sketch club had established a Cincinnati Art Club to "advance the knowledge and love of art through education." But membership was restricted to men.

Not to be left out or outdone, after just three organizational meetings, this efficient group of women laid out a new charter and elected four officers on December 10, 1892. The nineteen mostly single women—daughters of well-to-do families—were painters, potters, sculptors, wood carvers, and art teachers who had decided to devote their lives to art.

In less than a year, the new organization held with its first annual exhibition featuring 21 painters at Closson's. In the coming years, the Club set a nine-month schedule of painting subjects as a guide for members to present anonymously at juried competitions. At key moments in the early 20th century, members donated money for charitable causes, to pay teachers at the Art Academy, and to fund scholarships for Academy students.

In its more than 125 years of continuous operation—the oldest enduring arts association in the country—the Club has had several homes. Its permanent home (since 2006) is in Mariemont at the historic Resthaven Barn. A charitable foundation was established to raise money to purchase the barn, oversee its renovation, manage its operation, and develop the facility into the Woman's Art Club Cultural Center. Fondly called The Barn, the facility is used as office and exhibition space for Woman's Art Club members. Members contract with The Barn to teach classes or host workshops.

To commemorate its 125th anniversary, the Woman's Art Club partnered with ArtWorks to create a mural called *Emerge*. Designed by local artist Tina Westerkamp, the mural is on 12th Street between Race and Vine streets in OTR.

Today's members are versed in a broad array of fine arts and crafts, including piano and assorted instruments, voice, art-oriented travel, computer art, fashion design, product design, weaving, illustration, batik, dance, jewelry making, and more. Offerings include monthly meetings on the second Saturday of each month, September through May; three sponsored exhibitions per year; workshops, such as a three-day seminar on oil painting; and sponsorship of a scholarship program for arts education.

The Woman's Art Club encourages new members to join. Annual dues are $55.

—Kathy Merchant

Woman's Art Club Founders:

Christine Bredin	Clara Chipman Newton
Jennie Brookbank	Carlotta Agnes Raymond
Louise Fisher	Clemmie A. Roberts
Pauline Frank	Dixie Selden, secretary
Laura Fry, vice president	Mary Spencer, president
Altha Haydock (Caldwell)	Annie G. Sykes
Ida Holterhoff Holloway	Mary Trivett (Haight)
Grace Kennett	Henrietta Wilson,
(Wheelwright)	treasurer
Caroline Lord	Kate Wilson
Kate Reno Miller	

WOMEN'S ALLIANCE, INC. (1966)

The 1960s were turbulent times everywhere in the United States. Cincinnati was no exception. The city's Avondale neighborhood was particularly hard-hit following years of disinvestment and tension between the community and police.

A group of Cincinnati's leading African-American women—all educators and professionals—saw a crisis coming even before altercations in Avondale during 1967–68 were officially declared riots. They decided to take action, to do what was within their power to make a difference: expand the cultural, educational, and financial horizons of Cincinnati's underprivileged children and help instill pride in their lives.

It took the newly formed group a couple of years to settle on the best way to bring their vision to life. Initially, the organization responded to requests for small sums of money for community-building activities. Many of the requests for assistance came from teachers who were colleagues of the educator members of the Alliance. By 1971, the Women's Alliance had been fully persuaded through these requests to focus entirely on college scholarships, and youth-centered programs that encourage both career awareness and empowerment.

Then came the question of how to pay for the scholarships. Initially, Alliance members paid dues of $60 a month to support their charitable work. Fueled by even greater ambitions to have an impact on the educational future of Cincinnati's youth, and inspired by the idea of introducing the community to African-American artists, a marriage between education and art became the hallmark of the Women's Alliance.

In 1970, the Alliance launched partnerships with Cincinnati arts organizations featuring national African-American artists. Cincinnati Playhouse in the Park's *Ride a Black Horse* (Dr. John S. Scott, playwright) and *Five on the Black Hand Side* (written by Charlie L. Russell and starring Clarice Taylor) inaugurated the new series. Several years later, *One Mo' Time* (Vernel Bagneris, playwright) and *Sweet Honey & the Rock* (an all-woman, African-American a capella ensemble) were presented at the Taft Theatre. Notable national leaders including Julian Bond, Maya Angelou, and Susan Taylor have inspired youth in Cincinnati, and the Harlem Boys Choir was so popular that they visited Cincinnati's Music Hall twice in the early 1990s.

In recent years, the Alliance has invited many illustrious individuals and arts organizations to share in this partnership, including: poets Nikki Giovanni and Rita Dove, author and talk-show hostess Iyanla Vanzant, opera singer Desiree Dawson, Dayton Contemporary Dance Company, and talent shows featuring local students at The Carnegie.

The Alliance also sponsors annual fundraising activities, such as a holiday "Gift Giving Gala" to secure gifts and books for underprivileged children, a holiday shopping spree featuring 25+ African-American vendors held at the Kennedy Heights Art Center Lindner Annex, and the group's signature Hats Galore event to celebrate Jewels of the Community.

Since 1976, the Alliance has provided 240 college scholarships totaling $600,000.

—Kathy Merchant

Founding Members of the Women's Alliance, Inc.

Mary Curtis Ashong	Marcia Shaw*
Carol Braddock	Merri Gaither Smith
Cathy Buckhalter*	Evva Turpeau
Terri Embry	Gwen Wilder
Joellen Grady	
Pam Harshaw	*deceased

Chapter Three

21ST CENTURY CONTEMPORARY FOUNDERS

Cincinnati Baila! (2010)
Sandra Vazquez and Raquel Guillen
Clever Crazes for Kids (2006)
Dianne Dunkelman
concert:nova (2007)
Ixi Chen
FotoFocus (2010)
Mary Ellen Goeke
MamLuft&Co. Dance (2007)
Jeanne Mam-Luft

NrityArpana School of Performing Arts (2004)
Anupama Mirle
Triiibe (2017)
Siri Imani
Wave Pool (2014)
Calcagno Cullen
Young Professionals Choral Collective (2011)
KellyAnn Nelson

SANDRA VAZQUEZ & RAQUEL GUILLEN

Cincinnati Baila!

On a weekday night at a suburban Cincinnati dance studio, young students are showcasing their well-practiced steps and movements to their instructors and parents. That sentence could describe scores of local studios that offer dance classes.

But at Cincinnati Baila! in Blue Ash there are some key differences that set it apart.

For a start, four performing teenage girls wear traditional Mexican costumes. They hold up and raise outward long white dresses, twirling the delicate fabric while recorded music plays a folkloric dance, *son jarocho*, associated with Mexico's Veracruz state. Around their waists are *rebozos*, long red sashes tied like scarves, and they wear long necklaces. On their heads they balance glasses that shake a bit, the goal being to keep the glasses on their heads while dancing.

Cincinnati Baila!, founded in 2010, primarily teaches Mexican folkloric dances to children and teens, but has added flamenco, salsa, merengue and other dances, as well as adult classes. It was started by Raquel Guillen and Sandra Vazquez in Guillen's basement, but now has its own studio. The name translates from Spanish as "Cincinnati Dance!"

Vazquez and Guillen, who met in Cincinnati, have similar backgrounds. Both natives of Mexico City, they had studied and developed a love for their nation's dances as part of school cultural enrichment programs. Both have college degrees in something other than dance—Vazquez in graphic design and Guillen in chemical engineering. Their husbands worked for Procter & Gamble in Mexico and Venezuela before coming to Cincinnati.

Both women missed such cultural traditions as folkloric dance. "It is a very diverse place where culture is important," Guillen explains of Mexico. "People are very nationalist, but it is expressed mostly through culture. It's not only celebrating with the flag, it's about being proud of all the legacies we have."

At the time they met, both had young children. They worried about their children missing out on

Mexican folkloric dance. As they became involved with Cincinnati's Hispanic community, they learned that other parents had similar concerns.

Discussing that issue with friends over coffee, Vazquez recalls that she said, "Maybe I should start teaching my daughter—I know how to dance. (And) Raquel had exactly the same thinking about this." They resolved to have lessons in Spanish, as much as possible, and to offer classes to preschool children if they were ready.

Cincinnati Baila! primarily teaches girls, although boys are welcome since males traditionally have important roles in Mexican folkloric dance.

Cincinnati Baila! has become known throughout Cincinnati, thanks to public appearances by its students at the annual Cincy-Cinco Latino Festival, ArtsWave's Arts Sampler Weekend, and Cincinnati Symphony Orchestra's 2019 "Look Around" celebration at Washington Park. They have also performed before two past Mexican Presidents at Hispanic Chamber galas.

Vazquez and Guillen have created something far more than a dance studio for students and their parents. That is why, even though today they both have additional jobs, they look forward to Cincinnati Baila! becoming their full-time work.

"We are proud of how far along we are now," Vazquez says. "People like us that have Hispanic or biracial kids, or kids from another culture, feel they can come see other kids in families like theirs. So we are more than a dance academy, we are a community. We feel very happy about that—that was one of the purposes we were searching for."

—Steven Rosen

DIANNE DUNKELMAN

Clever Crazes for Kids

There is art all over the walls of Dianne Dunkelman's office. Big modern art with splashes of color, a glimpse of her personality. But there are also two signs that reveal more of her. One says "All In." The other says "Shine."

Neither alone would be an apt description of Dianne. But together, they fully encapsulate her life.

Dunkelman goes through the world looking for solutions to problems. If she cannot find one, she invents one. "Keep your heart and your head open," Dunkelman said. "The universe will give you what you need. All you have to do is be ready for it when it falls into your lap."

The driving forces for her can broadly be categorized into three groups: "Education, equity, and inclusion are everything to me." And the arts. Always the arts.

Dunkelman has supported the arts with her time, money, and optimism. If it seems like you recognize her name from a list of sponsors or board members, you do. She has served as a board member of Arts-Wave, Cincinnati Ballet, and Cincinnati Symphony Orchestra. She has helped raise tens of millions of dollars for the arts and health.

But her greatest passion, and not coincidentally her creativity, is reserved specifically for children and women's health.

Almost by accident, Dunkelman founded the National Speaking of Health Foundation in 1996. It began as a one-day women's health festival in Cincinnati. The event resonated with so many people that Speaking of Health spread across the country. The motto was: "Be strong. Be healthy. Be in charge." The program was such a stunning success that it was eventually acquired by the Cleveland Clinic Center for Specialized Women's Health, and continues today.

Much like her advocacy for helping women, Dianne's work to help children started small, but grew rather quickly.

Clever Crazes for Kids was formed in 2006 to be an asset for teachers, parents, kids, and guardians. Dunkelman knew that she needed to make things fun, free, and accessible. "What good is a program on a Saturday morning if a family is too poor to get the child there?"

She will work harder than anybody, but if she needs help, she will ask for it. Her optimism makes it easy. "Ask a favor, make a friend. People's basic nature is that they want to help." But she usually does not need much help. People are often surprised to learn that she goes to the office every day. She is surprised that they are surprised.

Clever Crazes is simple and effective, but a lot of work. The website is dynamic, popular and entirely free. Dunkelman wanted the instruction to be available online because that is where the children are. They didn't need an invitation.

The games for kids on the website (clevercrazes. com) teach kids reading, math, science, and the humanities. There are also lessons on financial literacy and ethics. What's not to like?

Most of the lessons were written by Dunkelman. When a guest arrives to her office, she hits play and speaks the words under her breath. Clever Crazes for Kids now gives away more than one million backpacks, books, and other gifts to school kids who could use a break. All of the backpacks are emblazoned with these three words: Smart. Strong. Cool. Dianne may need to get fitted for a monogrammed backpack. It's who she is.

—John Faherty

IXI CHEN

concert:nova

Ixi Chen doesn't usually play melody when she performs as a clarinetist with the Cincinnati Symphony Orchestra (CSO), and that's fine by her. Creating a harmonic accompaniment and a platform to amplify the voices of others is a theme threaded throughout her career.

Born in Taiwan, Chen's family moved to California when she was three to afford her greater access to all things, including the arts. She took dance, karate, musical theater, speed-reading—her parents wanted to expose her from a young age to everything America had to offer—even though they initially strongly discouraged her from studying music. Clearly, they eventually gave in.

Chen was a music major at UCLA before going on to graduate from the Manhattan School of Music, where she felt she could be more focused on music. While in New York, she worked as a telemarketer for the New York Philharmonic, and part of her compensation came in the form of free tickets to see the orchestra. She went twice a week, absorbing the details of orchestral performance, the nuances of the musicians, the energy they created on stage.

After graduation, Chen moved to Los Angeles to study in the acclaimed clarinetist Yehuda Gilad's studio. One semester in, she took an audition and moved to Germany. (She returned two years later to her studies with Gilad.) In Germany, she performed with a touring orchestra, an offshoot of the Schleswig-Holstein Music Festival. They played for the monarchs of Jordan, in Cairo, St. Petersburg, and Kiev, and in every nook and cranny of Germany.

While she was in Germany, Chen formed a small chamber group. (Earlier, in Los Angeles, she had also formed a chamber group.) Chen is drawn to the intimacy of music-making found in a small chamber group, and also to the ability to more fully derive the creative vision behind a piece. She would pick that passion back up in 2007, six years after she moved to Cincinnati to perform with the CSO, when she formed the chamber group concert:nova with other CSO musicians, including cellist and husband, Ted Nelson.

Concert:nova takes classical music into unexpected venues across the city, including bars and restaurants. The group thrives on collaboration, much like Chen. The ensemble's *Next:Generation* initiative provides education and experience for students from elementary school to the college-conservatory level. Chen also spends time as a teacher for the University of Cincinnati's College-Conservatory of Music and in private lessons.

Chen's career has taken her the world over and back again, and she has been able to follow her passion for music, both the melody and harmony, along the way.

—Leyla Shokoohe

MARY ELLEN GOEKE

FotoFocus

Like the photographers she champions, Mary Ellen Goeke prefers to work behind the lens. During a career of service to arts organizations across the East Coast and Midwest, Goeke has assembled powerful art exhibitions with an expert eye and a quiet efficiency.

As a co-founder and the founding executive director of Cincinnati's homage to lens-based art, FotoFocus, Goeke assumed that same role—building in the background—in an effort to expand the cultural dialogue around photography. She established one of the first major photography-focused organizations in the country to make grants to photographers. FotoFocus, which celebrates its 10th anniversary in 2020, has helped photography gain a prominent role in the modern art lexicon while also establishing Cincinnati as a key voice in the national conversation about the photographic medium.

In today's Instagram world, Goeke says, the art of photography has more relevance than ever. "Photography is such an immediate, fluid medium to work with now," she said. "It's inviting to young people. You create images in seconds. You can change them and manipulate them or destroy them or share them, and the process is so immediate."

The FotoFocus main event is its biennial, celebrated every other October. In 2020, Goeke expects the FotoFocus Biennial could grow to 100 venues and 250,000 visitors—up from 50 venues and 60,000 visitors in its first biennial year, 2012.

Born and raised in Northern Kentucky, Goeke graduated from the Art Academy of Cincinnati with a degree in painting and a minor in sculpture. She attended Bennington College in Vermont for post-graduate work in painting and then decided to pursue a career in museums. "As a child, I was taken to art classes at the Cincinnati Art Museum (CAM), and in my sophomore year of high school, we saw a Robert Ryman painting exhibition at the Contempo-

rary Art Center (CAC). I thought it was the coolest thing I had ever seen," she said. She was awarded the Elizabeth Nourse Painting Scholarship from the Art Academy in 1977.

In the early 1980s, while attending graduate studies in art history, Goeke served as a public information assistant at the CAC. In 1984, she moved to the CAM as an assistant registrar. In the late 1980s, she served as the head registrar for the American Federation of the Arts, a New York City-based consortium of museums that organizes national exhibits. From there, she became head registrar at Wadsworth Atheneum Museum of Art in Hartford, Connecticut.

Millard Rogers, then director of the Cincinnati Art Museum, brought her home in 1993 to serve as head of exhibitions. In 1997, she moved to Chicago to join the Terra Museum of American Art, and a few years later, she was back in Cincinnati working as a consultant with the CAC and the Underground Railroad Freedom Center. She joined forces with Tom Schiff and James Crump as they were beginning to conceptualize FotoFocus as a photography festival.

"I've always been a person who liked working on the mechanics of a project in existing museums," she said. "What I find inspiring about what we do at FotoFocus is that we provide the funding for people's curatorial projects."

Much like the nature of photography itself, she said, "I find working to start a nonprofit that helps fund photographers, and diverse and timely curatorial choices, gives me immediate gratification."

—Carolyn Pione Micheli

CINCINNATI BALLET "BOLD MOVES" (2017)

JEANNE MAM-LUFT

MamLuft&Co. Dance

The work of choreographer Jeanne Mam-Luft is often inspired by her experiences as a refugee and memories shared by her parents, who escaped the Cambodian genocide before her birth.

Her latest dance project might be the most auto-biographical she has created among the more than 30 in her portfolio.

The founder of MamLuft&Co. Dance in 2007, Mam-Luft's newest work springs from historical events in 1970. A military coup felled the ruling Cambodian monarch. The Khmer Rouge, a brutal communist regime attempting to create a master race through social engineering, formed an alliance with the deposed king leading to five years of civil war. On April 30, President Richard Nixon announced the American invasion of Cambodia. It sparked renewed war protests on campuses across the United States, including at Kent State University in northern Ohio.

Envisioned while recently an artist-in-residence at Kent State, this new piece is an attempt to synthesize events that shaped her life, including her parents' arranged marriage by the Khmer Rouge. Her family's story can't help but inform the work.

"They separated families, sent children to be brainwashed. Young people like my parents were sent to work camps," she said. "Ninety percent of the writers, artists, and academics were killed. My grandfather was executed. My father, who was principal of a school, was not killed because he had value to build irrigation systems."

When the Khmer Rouge and dictator Pol Pot lost power in 1979, Mam-Luft's parents and her then 1-year-old sister were among the masses fleeing northwest to Thailand. Baby Jeanne was born in 1980 in a refugee camp, and the family was soon allowed to enter the U.S. as refugees.

Brought up in suburban Dallas in a large community of Cambodian and Vietnamese refugees, Mam-Luft was a gifted student who was interested in arts but did not start dancing until high school. "You're told, 'If you're a teen it's too late to start,' but I went ahead," she said. "It was transformative. It connected to who I was in ways I couldn't verbalize. I couldn't stop dancing. I needed to breathe. It grounded me and set me free at the same time."

Despite her love of dance and interest in it as a career, she accepted a scholarship to study architecture at Carnegie Mellon University in Pittsburgh, where she met the man she would later marry and who would bring her to southwest Ohio. In the meantime, she earned a master's degree in fine arts at Texas Woman's University, writing her thesis about the presence of design in dance.

She and her husband, a percussionist with the Dayton Philharmonic, settled in Cincinnati. Mam-Luft said she worked two "soul-sucking" years as an architect. She founded her dance company in 2007, infusing her choreography with her architectural expertise.

"In 1970, my parents were the same ages as my students. The dancers in my professional company aren't much older. In 1970, these people experienced horrific events, but life continues. You make a choice to become an artist and try to answer questions. 'I am in this country, why? Why didn't I die? Why did all of my relatives live different lives on less than a dollar a day in Cambodia? I always had a lot of guilt.' "

—Mark Curnutte

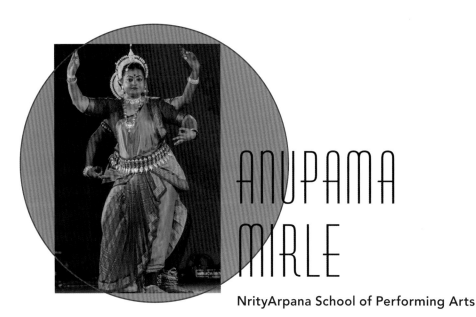

ANUPAMA MIRLE

NrityArpana School of Performing Arts

Anupama (Anupa) Mirle can't remember when during her childhood she started dancing. She believes it was about when she started walking. Fortunately for Mirle, the region where she grew up in South India nurtured a strong tradition of classical Indian dance.

The 1960s was a time in India when classical dance was considered show business as a holdover from British colonial times. But with her mother's encouragement, young Anupa Rao whirled, twirled and ultimately stepped gracefully into that tradition as she learned to master classic dances.

Mirle's love of dance has also turned out to be fortunate for Cincinnati. She teaches it from her non-profit NrityArpana School of Performing Arts studio in the northern suburb of West Chester. Mirle and her dancers also share their talents in regional events such as Arts Sampler programs sponsored by Arts-Wave, Asian Fest, and the Indian Film Festival.

Mirle initially came to the U.S. to study chemistry, went on to earn an MBA, and worked for Procter & Gamble in Maryland. Twenty years ago, she landed in Cincinnati when her husband, also a chemist, was offered a job with Procter & Gamble.

Soon after their arrival in Cincinnati, Mirle said, she began to miss the dancing she had learned and practiced for many years. And she missed the cultural connections that it nurtures. So when she and her husband planned their new suburban home, they included a basement dance floor where she could indulge her love of the art.

News of her interest in dance spread to the parents of her son's school friends, and the interest was contagious in the region's Indian community. She began to teach Indian classical dance in her basement, but it soon proved too small to contain the strong interest from both youngsters and adults. In 2004, Mirle opened the NrityArpana School of Performing Arts.

Since the school's opening, Mirle estimates that she has taught dance to several hundred people, mostly girls and women, although she has had some male students learning a form of classical Indian dancing called Bharatanatyam. NrityArpana students come from all over the area and are mostly of Indian ancestry. Mirle is devoted to preserving the heritage of Indian classical dance, but also wants to expose audiences to people who are not like themselves.

Anyone who has seen classical Indian dancing knows it is a fantastical mix of motion, music, and vivid colors. Mirle compares Indian classical dancing's imprint on Indian culture to ballet's place in Western culture. She said it also carries on a folk tradition that has existed for centuries in India. The colorful costumes worn by the NrityArpana dancers must come from India. "No one in the U.S. is making them now so we have to order them. They are an essential part of what we do."

Mirle and her school's influence on the Cincinnati region's cultural life is immeasurable. As an arts advocate, Mirle was instrumental in bringing a UNESCO program called World Dance Day to Cincinnati in 2009. As an ambassador for sharing beauty and diversity who was recognized for her work in 2013 as an Ohio Arts Council Heritage Fellow, Mirle says "I feel that it is important to enable many bridges and dialogues between groups. But ultimately, relating to people as individuals and not a group creates a more sustainable and harmonious society."

—Dave Caudill

SIRI
IMANI

Triiibe

Even a short conversation with Siri Imani can go in multiple directions: verbal arts, poetry, urban gardening, community service and building, music, technology, video production, and basketball and kickball.

Though only entering her mid-20s, Imani has emerged as a true renaissance woman on Cincinnati's cultural scene.

A former basketball star and big-college recruit at Withrow High School under her given name, Siri Huey, Imani is one of the organizers of Triiibe. It is a 13-member group of black artists creating music, video and other accurate expressions of urban culture while providing community-wide enrichment programs that are primarily focused on youth ages nine to nineteen. Triiibe is an acronym that stands for True Representation of Intellectual Individuals Invoking Black Excellence. They're all under 30.

Three members of the larger Triiibe collective comprise a hip-hop group that performs original music and lyrics and can be heard on streaming services such as Spotify. Triiibe released its second album, "III Am What III Want to Be," late last year. Its music has entered the Chicago market and earned a handful of Cincinnati-based honors. Imani is the group's poet/lyricist, Aziza Love its songstress, and PXVCE (pronounced Peace) a musician.

"Triiibe the collective is an era, us doing enrichment things none of us had growing up," Imani said during a 2019 interview in the Main Branch of the Public Library of Cincinnati and Hamilton County. The no-cost program Raising the Bar—an introduction to visual and audio arts—was about to begin in the library's nearby Teen Center. It's one of Triiibe's signature youth arts programs. The library is a partner with Cincinnati Public Schools, a number of schools outside the city, and the nonprofit Elementz Hip Hop youth organization.

Triiibe also has urban gardens and provides a once-a-month dinner for people experiencing home-lessness, called Potluck for the People, in Piatt Park. Besides food, free clothing and personal hygiene products are available. Triiibe's volunteerism in Cincinnati schools revealed how many children were hungry, many of them residents of the Walnut Hills area, and moved Triiibe members to enroll in urban gardening classes to learn how to manage plots and grow food.

The eclectic nature of Triiibe, its desire to help and willingness to learn, all are reflections of Imani. Born to a mother who is a poet, Imani developed a love of words as a child. Then it was all basketball. She excelled at hauling in rebounds from missed shots. She said she was supposed to be in the WNBA by now if not for a series of injuries. Even at a muscled 5'10", her body could not withstand the continual pounding under the basket. Forced to give up basketball after a short career at Lake Michigan College, Imani said, "I had to reimagine who I am and what my life was about."

Yet her mind was sharp. She found fulfillment in writing and performing, bursting onto the scene by speaking her original and sprawling *Lost Generation* poem at a Black Lives Matter rally in July 2016. Imani's message there, as it is in her larger work with Triiibe, is as deeply personal as it is universal:

*We're a generation losing hope, but we're
    not hopeless.
Some of us are out here trying to fight for what
    we believe in, and no one seems to notice.
Instead of having our backs, they go behind it
    and scold us.
Instead of telling us what to do, why don't you
    stand up and show us?*

                    —Mark Curnutte

CALCAGNO CULLEN

Wave Pool

A credible practice of socially engaged art requires years to build. To think it can be achieved in a short period of time and without personal immersion is disrespectful of the community.

In the five years since they opened Wave Pool in a former fire station in the Camp Washington neighborhood, Calcagno Cullen and her husband, Geoffrey Cullen, have completely invested themselves.

The couple, their daughter, and their dog live in the Wave Pool building on Colerain Avenue not far from Interstate 75. They've attracted a bookseller they met in San Francisco and drew him to Camp Washington, where he has opened the Fringe book stand in a shed beside his house.

Wave Pool owns a second building which houses a program in which immigrants and refugees can form a community and sell their art and jewelry. An adjacent space in that building was in the process of rehabilitation in late 2019 to create a teaching kitchen for at-risk people—including new arrivals to Cincinnati—with a goal of pairing chefs from those communities with artists. The kitchen, workspace and shop are part of Wave Pool's Welcome Project, a social enterprise designed to empower people in these marginalized populations.

"We have credibility as artists when we make something that is greater than the sum of its parts, when we combine assets and connect people to make these things a little more magical," said Cullen, a 2004 Miami University graduate who went on to earn a master's degree in fine art from the University of Cincinnati College of Design, Architecture, Art, and Planning (DAAP). She is trained as a painter.

"As social practitioners, we believe in making something with other people. I am the person I am to serve. I walk the dog three times a day. I meet people on the street and invite them to the gallery. The art process is collaborative," she said. And she and her husband have done exactly that. They've partnered with inmates at River City Correctional Center in the center's urban farm project and with the nearby American Sign Museum.

Inside of their converted fire house is a traditional gallery and wood shop that offers time slots during the week for the public to use. Wave Pool's wood shop program is managed by woodworker Scott Bellissemo and its Welcome Project by Erika Allen. Ceramics classes are taught by a rotation of three ceramicists. A show titled *Home Makers* at the Wave Pool gallery in Fall 2019 highlighted pieces created in those programs, along with a workshop in pretzel baking, poetry readings, and puppet shows. "We do have more traditional exhibits with paintings on the walls that get analyzed by historians," Cullen said.

Yet community is the focus, and for all of the upsides, there are downsides to running a community-based arts project in a historically under served and impoverished community. "There is drug dealing and sex work on the corner," Cullen said. "I wonder sometimes how long Wave Pool is going to be around. It's not healthy for an organization to be run by one voice for too long. We might need to have a new executive director every eight to ten years. We're sustainable, we're not in danger of shutting down. We just face a lot of challenges."

—Mark Curnutte

KELLYANN NELSON

Young Professionals Choral Collective

In the Cincinnati choral community, KellyAnn Nelson is akin to the Beatles. Such is the zeal participants have for her ensemble, the Young Professionals Choral Collective (affectionately referred to as YPCC).

An alumna of Western Michigan University for both undergraduate and master's degrees, Nelson also studied for her doctorate in choral conducting at the University of Cincinnati before leaving Ohio in the early 2000s. Fate had not a small hand in bringing Nelson back to Cincinnati. After hearing her presentation at a national children's chorus forum held in Cincinnati, now-husband Christopher Eanes offered her a role as education director for the Cincinnati Boychoir. (Nelson went on to serve as the managing artistic director of the organization for several years.)

YPCC began in 2011 as a way to engage young professionals in Cincinnati during the World Choir Games, which were held here in the summer of 2012. Having just recently moved to the city, Nelson found a rehearsal space at Below Zero on Walnut Street, a bar with a piano that was free on Tuesday nights, which is when she wanted to gather. She put out a call on Facebook for YPs looking to participate, and around 40 people showed up to the first-ever meeting. The next week, that number doubled. A concert followed two months later, and then the World Choir Games (where the fledgling YPCC took home second place in their division).

The value proposition for YPCC was different than anything Cincinnati had seen. Here was an op-portunity for creative expression with like-minded individuals from all walks of life. Many participants were looking for a place to fit in, a tribe. Nelson found a way to engage young professionals by first understanding what was important to them. The singers remain the central focus of YPCC, rather than on the types of productions that could fill the most seats—a bold and refreshing move in artistic consideration. The number of singers has ballooned to over 1,200.

Concerts take place in cycles: six to eight weeks of Tuesday night rehearsals precede a large themed performance, typically featuring more than 150 singers, in iconic venues across the city. For example, members of YPCC performed with the Cincinnati Opera in sold-out performances of Blind Injustice (2019). They also perform in iconic venues in other parts of the country. Nelson conducted a YPCC concert in New York's Carnegie Hall during the summer of 2019.

It turns out that 2019 was a pivotal year for Nelson and her family. They moved to Washington, D.C., and Nelson took on a new role as advertising and development associate with the national organization Chorus America. She remains the artistic director of YPCC for the 2019–2020 season while the organization seeks someone to fill her groundbreaking shoes.

—Leyla Shokoohe

Chapter Four

CONTEMPORARY WOMEN

Diane Carr
Shannon Carter
Jan Brown Checco
Alva Jean Crawford
Kathryne Gardette
Janelle Gelfand
Nikki Giovanni
Amy Goodwin
Robin Guarino
Heather Hallenberg
Barbara Kellar
Tammy Kernodle
Pam Kravetz
Quiera Levy-Smith
Rhoda Mayerson
Dr. Carolyn L. Mazloomi
Constance McClure

Mary McCullough-Hudson
Ellen Muse-Lindeman
Jeaunita Olówè
Melody Sawyer Richardson
Annie Ruth
Ann Santen
Rosemary Schlachter
Kristen Schlotman
Rebecca "Reba" Senske
Marie Speziale
Mary Stagaman
Toilynn O'Neal Turner
Sandy Underwood
Diana Vandergriff-Adams
Angela Powell Walker
Ginger Warner
Kathy Y. Wilson

DIANE CARR

Diane Carr has multiple academic degrees and a work history that includes classroom teacher, communications and marketing in corporate America, and director and costume designer at College-Conservatory of Music at the University of Cincinnati.

Those experiences, though, were setting the stage for her grand finale. Beginning in 2004, Carr would spend the next 15 years designing and piloting a program that would bring musical theater and sustainable arts programs to thousands of students in under-served middle schools across the country.

Carr led the development of JumpStart Theatre while working as an executive at the Cincinnati-based Educational Theatre Association (EdTA). It is a program that comes with a three-year grant that enables a middle school to mount a musical production. Carr said JumpStart is referred to as *Annie* in a Box and is modeled after a program in New York City.

"The idea was to create sustainability and a groundswell in the community to create a theater program," Carr said. The pilot started in the Cincinnati area in 2015, and now six local schools—Holmes Middle, Gamble Montessori, Finneytown Middle, Aiken New Tech, Dater High, and Felicity-Franklin Middle—have self-sustaining musical theater programs. At Gamble, the music teacher collaborated with a reading and a social studies teacher to take on the JumpStart model. Carr said that arrangement reminded her of her first teaching job at Bellevue High School in 1974 when she coached softball and oversaw the pep club because no one else would. "It ties into what I've done the past 15 years. I have vision for how people can work together."

Three additional local schools began their three-year JumpStart process in 2019–2020 along with schools in St. Louis, San Diego, Atlanta, and Frostburg,

Maryland. The Children's Theatre of Cincinnati is the local company that oversees JumpStart in this area.

Research shows many positive effects from JumpStart participation on student development and behavior in areas such as critical thinking and outlook on the future. Besides building sustainable programs, JumpStart aims to engage as many students as possible in all aspects of theater and prepare students for high school and beyond by instilling collaboration, communication, and problem-solving skills.

"You build a sense of community, build friendships and build success," said Carr, who has had no problem selling JumpStart's benefits. She wrote her dissertation on the effects that school-based arts programs have on parental involvement for her Ph.D. in Educational Leadership in 2018 at Northern Kentucky University. She then produced a volunteer guide for JumpStart on "all the jobs parents could do in a musical," she said. Under Carr's leadership, JumpStart generated $1 million in donations for support and expansion.

Yet leading JumpStart's development wasn't the only major achievement in her years with Educational Theatre Association. As its director of chapter relations and community engagement, Carr helped to build EdTA volunteer organizations in 48 states and was involved in promoting excellence in student theater in high schools through EdTA's International Thespian Society.

—Mark Curnutte

SHANNON CARTER

As a child, Shannon Carter, née Kelly, delighted in trick-or-treating at the home of local philanthropist Patricia Corbett. "There were so few kids on the street, my brothers and I would go home and change our costumes to go back for more candy!" said Carter.

She credits her relationship with Corbett, other influential family friends, and especially her parents with the development of her deep philanthropic spirit.

It was during her time as an art major at Boston College that Carter enjoyed numerous shopping trips to Boston's fashion mecca, Newberry Street. There she discovered The Shop for Pappagallo and decided—along with a business partner—to open a Cincinnati site at the age of 22. To save money, Carter hand-drew the advertising and marketing materials, including a 4"x 6" recipe booklet to promote sales.

In 1979, Carter married Lee Ault Carter. She describes their relationship as one of "kindred spirits." They were both raised in families who were very philanthropic and community focused. Lee Carter was a member of the Fine Arts Fund board (now ArtsWave). Shannon Carter's education and interest in the arts was a perfect fit. When Shannon Carter was named a Great Living Cincinnatian in 2015, the couple was described as "practically a package deal."

Carter felt fortunate to be able to count among their early mentors several senior and influential members of the community. "We weren't that significant at the time," says Carter, "but we learned from the best. We had the Corbetts, the Lazarus', and the Rosenthals, and as younger folks, learning from the best felt really good."

In 1986, the Carters co-chaired Cincinnati's first Fine Arts Fund Sampler Weekend, a free public showcase highlighting local theaters, dance, museums, music, festivals, and performances. Carter also chaired the Cincinnati Antiques Festival that year, as well as significant fundraising events for the Taft Museum of Art. Cincinnati's Best Kept Secrets, a signature event benefiting the Cincinnati Ballet, was a day-long home, garden, and entertaining fair.

Carter's creativity and community focus led her to found Crayons to Computers (C2C) in 1997 after developing the concept of a teacher resource center with a seven-member team during Leadership Cincinnati (Class XIX). She led the organization for 16 years as volunteer executive director. Since its inception, C2C has distributed more than $163 million of free school supplies and has inspired similar programs in 42 other cities.

Neophytes to the choir world, the Carters took on the task of co-chairing the World Choir Games (WCG) in 2012. Instead of a traditional PowerPoint pitch, the pair took a creative approach to fundraising at a Queen City Club event. Members of The Southern Gateway Choir were engaged to masquerade as servers. As the Carters listed the types of music that would be performed at the WCG, the servers burst into song as a barbershop quartet. The remaining members of the choir joined in, and in complete harmony sang for 25 minutes. "Everyone was toe-tapping, grinning from ear-to-ear, and we raised hundreds of thousands of dollars," recalls Carter.

As a result of the critical role that more than 4,000 volunteers played in the success of the WCG, Carter co-founded the Welcomers Community Volunteer Network of Cincinnati USA/ Northern Kentucky, which today continues to provide world-class hospitality to visitors attending national and international arts, cultural, and special events.

—Ilene Ross Tucker

JAN BROWN CHECCO

Jan Brown Checco has transformed what it means to convene, collaborate, and connect through art. Specializing in project design and directing public works projects, she has 24 years of experience as an arts administrator and 45 years as a studio artist.

Her work and contributions laid the foundation for the flourishing community art we see in Cincinnati today. Checco's belief that art is a critical form of communication that removes barriers and enables mutual respect drives the indelible impact of her work on those involved in creating it, and on the city that benefits from her creative spirit.

Growing up as a Cincinnati native, daughter of a classical pianist and an engineer, Checco's love of art stemmed from relationships with her grandmother, a milliner and dressmaker, and her uncle, a marketing professor who traveled extensively. Instilled with an open mind and a desire to create, Checco's approach balances art with science and reason with intuition.

Perhaps the most formative element came in the form of her "art mother," Constance McClure, a Cincinnati Art Academy professor who pioneered the use of esoteric media in the face of adversity and criticism. Connie legitimized Checco's use of her family as a subject, validating her artwork and inspiring portraits of her children that remain among her proudest accomplishments today.

In a twist of fate, Checco met some international engineers while ushering as a volunteer at Playhouse in the Park. Leveraging rudimentary French, she helped them to their seats and started a relationship that resulted in her moving to Paris in 1980 to pursue her dreams as an artist. Checco immediately connected with P&G's European Art Director, which led to her contributing to two of the largest publishing houses, designing postage stamps, and conceptualizing album record jackets for RCA.

She also met her lifelong partner in enabling good in the world, Gérald Checco, who has become an important leader in Cincinnati's city administration. Five years in Paris brought work, growth, and love in the form of marriage and two young daughters.

Returning to Finneytown, Checco delivered her first big art collaboration from 1994–1996 with Art on the Square, an international art festival bringing together over 10,000 visitors and hundreds of artists. She led the 2006 Vine Street Mural campaign. Working with local teens to restore street waste cans and create movable art murals applied to vacant OTR buildings, Checco set the precedent for all other Cincinnati neighborhood mural programs.

As a Cincinnati Parks Board art administrator, Checco designed the International Butterfly Shows from 2007–2012, delighting the city and driving cultural understanding. Her most notable art accomplishment occurred in 2003 with *Clay, Color and Fire*, an international artist exchange project bringing together master ceramics artists from eight cities to create a permanent handmade tile installation at the Pavilion in Friendship Park. This work of art symbolizes her ability to bring people together and create lasting legacies. Checco is a true master artist of convening and connecting, enabling Cincinnati and the broader world to be a better place.

"A good artist lets intuition lead him wherever it wants. A good scientist has freed himself of concepts and keeps his mind open to what is…"—Lao-Tzu, Tao te Ching

—Christi Geary

ALVA JEAN CRAWFORD

Alva Jean Crawford is one of those rare people who can use both sides of her brain in equal measure. She is very good at connecting head and heart. Crawford's 22-year career as a math teacher, plus ten years as a school counselor, has centered on one goal.

That goal has been encouraging students to pursue an education that can lead to a successful adult life. Her passion for Cincinnati's arts in retirement borders on that level of devotion.

Born in Memphis, Tennessee, Crawford moved to Cincinnati in 1977 when her husband, Alvin, became chairman of the Orthopedics Department at Cincinnati Children's Hospital Medical Center. In recognition of their gifts of time and talent—individually and as a couple—both Crawfords have been named Great Living Cincinnatians by the Cincinnati USA Regional Chamber. Crawford was also recognized in 2005 as an *Enquirer* Woman of the Year.

As part of her 2019 recognition, the Chamber shared a story that reveals Crawford's sturdy, yet gentle, nature: "Crawford was the first African American ticket agent in the mid-South. She was asked to apply for the position when American Airlines decided it was time for racial integration. She got the job after a test and an interview. 'People used to watch me work like I was something strange' said Crawford. 'It was good to open the opportunities for African Americans…but it was not my career goal, so I left after two years.' "

With a special passion for the Cincinnati Opera, Crawford has held many volunteer leadership roles: secretary of the Board of Trustees; co-chair of the 80th Anniversary Gala in 2000 and the 2019 Gala "Love Letters to Patty" (Beggs); chair of the Diversity, Equity & Inclusion Committee; and the search for artistic director Evans Mirageas. She co-chaired the steering committee that commissioned *Margaret Garner* based on the real-life experiences of a runaway slave. According to Crawford in a *Cincinnati Magazine* feature, "We were a very diverse group, and we all had to talk about our feelings about doing this. It was hard for some of us."

Other arts-related pursuits include Cincinnati Ballet's diversity committee, the board of Cincinnati Playhouse in the Park, and the board of the Music Hall Revitalization Company. As a Great Living Cincinnatian, Crawford said "My desired contribution is to encourage others, regardless of their personal circumstances, to enjoy the arts and realize that diversity and inclusion is good for us all."

Crawford's board service in the community is diverse and encyclopedic, including Greater Cincinnati Foundation, Cincinnati Public Radio, Free Store Foodbank, and Cincinnati Woman's Club. She also mentors students for Cincinnati Youth Collaborative, the Major League Baseball Academy, and Cincinnati Woman's Club, and provides math tutoring at several Cincinnati Public Schools.

Crawford's words to live by are deeply held: do unto others as you would have them do unto you. Period. Treat others as if they are your family and friends, and do not judge. "It's what's inside that really matters. I like to help anybody who needs help. It doesn't matter who or what they are. We all want the same things for our families and friends." And if we all did that, well, it might be a better world.

Even with such expansive community devotion, there's still time for fun in Crawford's life, including her grandchildren, tennis, classes at OLLI and the Cincinnati Woman's Club, music and theater, reading, and world travel. It's a full and satisfying life.

—Kathy Merchant

KATHRYNE GARDETTE

Kathryne Gardette has a knack for finding the prime parking spot on McMillan Avenue just a few feet from the front door of one of her favorite Walnut Hills neighborhood spots, Caffe Vivace.

She had been there just a few nights earlier to listen to live jazz while working on her traditional fiber art. Gardette creates accessories with adinkra message symbols from the West African nation of Ghana. In fact, she wore one that winter morning on her white sweater. In two shades of purple, geometric, framed with small stones, the image stands for civic responsibility. It's not just a piece of jewelry. It describes a way of life. Her way of life.

"It is my responsibility to help build up my community. It is my responsibility to be engaged in government," said Gardette, as she settled in at a table to share her story. She paused, and then said, "We are all connected."

Connection, civic responsibility, community, the arts, a broker of positive energy, these are the traits that make up Kathryne Gardette. She was president (again) in 2019 of the Walnut Hills Area Council, the neighborhood's official representative organization at Cincinnati City Hall. She is a member of Cincinnati Public Schools strategic planning committee and volunteers at her neighborhood school, Frederick Douglass. She is a former president of the Walnut Hills Redevelopment Foundation and was known for leading community events or board meetings that lasted long into the night.

A few city blocks to the west of Caffe Vivace is the building that she owns with her husband, Baba Charles Miller, a professional percussionist. Gardette can be found there on Monday mornings and Thursday nights participating in regular mindfulness sessions.

That is now. This was then: in 1996, she helped to create ArtWorks, which puts young artists to work each summer painting magnificent murals on city walls. The first was in Walnut Hills. She and her husband volunteered as teaching artists for ArtWorks' first performance project, Drums for Peace. She was a founding member of the Cincinnati Arts Association Diversity Committee and was vice president of the nonprofit organization Learning Through Art. "It's not a list," Gardette said. "It's what I do."

She's not only a community volunteer. She has made time for those activities while working a day job in logistics and marketing for Prestige AV & Creative Services. She's academically qualified. She has a master's of science degree in Positive Organization Development Change from Case Western Reserve University in Cleveland. She embodies the degree's listing in the course catalog to empower "experienced professionals to affect positive change in diverse spheres of influence—balancing economic well-being, social responsibility and environmental sustainability."

Gardette has brought it all to Walnut Hills. As a child growing up in Evanston, it's where she would come to shop at Ebony Records and Thatch Root for African clothing and jewelry. She smiled in telling how she always looks up to see the illuminated ArtWorks' installation *Campground* at the Cincinnati Art Museum when driving north on Gilbert Avenue after a trip across town or across the country. "It lets me know I'm home."

—Mark Curnutte

JANELLE GELFAND

For over 26 years, Janelle Gelfand was the voice of music and the arts for the *Cincinnati Enquirer*. The San Francisco Bay Area native began her career at the paper in 1991, first as an arts critic, and very soon (1993) as a specialist critic for classical music.

During her lengthy tenure, Gelfand traveled with the Cincinnati Symphony Orchestra on three extensive European tours, as well as two trips to Japan, and accompanied the Cincinnati Pops on their first-ever visit to Mainland China and Singapore.

Corporate changes at the *Enquirer* in 2017 left Gelfand to search quickly for a new outlet for her work. Her departure occurred just before the grand re-opening of Cincinnati Music Hall's major renovation project, a story Gelfand had been covering extensively. In only two weeks, and just in time to cover the opening, Cincinnati Public Radio station WGUC provided a home for Gelfand's blog called *Janelle's Notes* as well as a radio spot on its sister station WVXU-FM.

"Bringing Janelle's blog to wguc.org will provide a wider audience for her respected performance reviews, personality profiles, and features on the region's arts organizations and thought leaders, and will continue WGUC's longtime commitment to the region's arts community," said Richard Eiswerth, president and general manager of Cincinnati Public Radio.

In addition to being an accomplished journalist, Gelfand is a classically trained pianist. She has a bachelor's degree in music from Stanford University, a master's degree in Piano Performance, and a doctorate in musicology from the University of Cincinnati College-Conservatory of Music, where she was also an instructor in music history for three years. "I'm a musicologist and a performing pianist," says Gelfand. "I have always felt from both sides of the aisle I could identify with the performers because I know what has gone into preparing."

We invited Gelfand to share, in her own words, recollections of international travels with the Cincinnati Symphony Orchestra (edited for brevity):

"In the beginning, I was not allowed to ride the bus with the musicians. I had to get myself from city to city, get my own plane tickets, everything, because of union rules. Then they voted that I could sit on their bus to get from Tokyo to Yokahama, but I had to sit with the PR person in the front. I was the first person to send reviews (to Cincinnati) over the internet from Europe. In the beginning, most of the hotels I stayed in never had (internet service because) WiFi wasn't (yet) invented. I remember going to an all-night internet café in a really seedy district, writing my review, and finishing it at 2 am. Then I had to figure out how to get back to my hotel on the other side of the Seine."

"I was (also) the first person to blog from China. China was kind of a sketchy situation because at the time they didn't like journalists, so I contacted the state department and they told me 'don't write journalist, just put down PR with the symphony.' So, I actually lied on my visa, which made me more nervous. I was so glad when we left China. We had to wipe my computer clean of anything that said *Enquirer*, or newspaper, and I sent everything to an unmarked Yahoo account. It was crazy. Looking back, I'm positive I was being watched, but it was an adventure."

—Ilene Ross Tucker

NIKKI GIOVANNI

On April 17, 2007, the nation's eyes were fixed on Nikki Giovanni. Not because of her volumes of poetry. Not because of her fiery prose. Not because she's a literary luminary with a half century of awards to her name.

The country was watching her—a small, slight figure behind the podium in Cassell Coliseum on the campus of Virginia Tech—because the day before, a student had gone on a rampage and killed 32 people.

The country was waiting for her to articulate something meaningful before a silent, sorrowful crowd—students, faculty, reporters with their photographers, President George W. Bush with the First Lady. And so she delivered her first line: "We are Virginia Tech."

Nikki Giovanni's address that closed the memorial convocation—a mere 258 words, written just hours after the massacre—was a symphony of comfort, resilience, defiance, and pride. And when it was over the audience, so mute just moments before, exploded with applause.

Where did that message come from? How does a writer wring courage from such a tragedy?

"I sat at my computer," she recalls. "And the only thing I could think of was: We are Virginia Tech—not this thing that has happened to us." After that, she says, "It just started to flow."

So many words have flowed from Yolande Cornelia "Nikki" Giovanni. Her work as a poet, writer, activist, and educator have earned innumerable honors, including the Langston Hughes Medal and seven NAACP Image Awards. She was the first recipient of the Rosa Parks Women of Courage Award, and Oprah Winfrey has named her a Living Legend.

Her parents moved to Cincinnati from Knoxville, Tennessee, settling first in Wyoming, then Lincoln Heights. Nikki was a child; it would be years before she grasped the indignity of the city's whites-only lunch counters or the injustice of segregated schools.

But her parents knew. When Emmitt Till was murdered, one of her older sister's teachers said that the boy deserved it. Her dad and three other fathers confronted the teacher and made her apologize.

Nikki went to live with her grandparents and attend high school in Knoxville, graduating from Fisk University with honors. In the summer of 1967, she was back in Cincinnati, where she organized the city's first black arts festival. Her plan to get a degree in social work was derailed when a faculty member recognized her writing talent and steered her to Columbia University's MFA program.

In 1968 she self-published her first poetry collection, *Black Feelings, Black Talk*, and by the early 1970s she was a leading voice in the Black Arts Movement. Her uncompromising African-American perspective continued as she expanded into children's literature, essay-writing, and public speaking.

In the mid-1980s she briefly returned to Cincinnati, teaching at the College of Mount St. Joseph (now Mt. St. Joseph University). And in 1995 a diagnosis of lung cancer brought her back to the city for surgery that, she says, saved her life.

She joined the faculty of Virginia Tech in 1987 and continues there today as a University Distinguished Professor. In her most recent work *A Good Cry: What We Learn from Tears and Laughter*, she offers an intimate look at her personal history. Now, at 76, she is listening to the nation's new voices.

"I was out weeding the other day and I thought to myself, I've done all I know how to do to help the flowers grow," she says. "There's another generation that has to make up its mind."

—Linda Vaccariello

AMY GOODWIN

Cincinnati has seen an explosion of new arts-oriented community events and civic engagement movements recently, and it will be hard to find one that hasn't benefited from a relationship with the Johnson Foundation and its president and CEO, Amy Goodwin.

BLINK, MusicNOW, People's Liberty, Washington Park, ArtWorks, Contemporary Arts Center, and Ensemble Theatre Cincinnati all count her as a friend and supporter.

Since 2012, when Goodwin took over the foundation launched by distant relatives, she's focused on strengthening the vibrancy of Cincinnati's urban core through thoughtful grantmaking. Though she's not able to give truly game-changing grant amounts, Goodwin uses the foundation's assets strategically to promote equity and inclusion. "I've supported the arts, of course, because the arts are such a big part of why Cincinnati is so exciting right now," she says. "There are no other U.S. cities our size with the inclusive arts scene we have."

In her first years with the Johnson Foundation, Goodwin partnered with the Haile/U.S. Bank Foundation to create such transformative community engagement programs as People's Liberty, which funded individuals seeking to improve their communities (many were performing and visual artists), and LumenoCity, the multi-year light show celebration with the Cincinnati Symphony Orchestra that helped raise awareness of Music Hall's renovation needs. The Johnson Foundation also provided funding for the first BLINK festival from the creative team behind LumenoCity.

Goodwin recruited a new generation of donors, dubbed The 50, to help the Contemporary Arts Center (CAC) institute free admission following its lobby renovation. The Johnson Foundation contributed $25,000 per year for three years, and 50 individuals—most of whom had never donated to the arts—committed to giving $1,000 each year over the same period. CAC attendance doubled, and a new wave of Cincinnati philanthropists were born. "These folks, mostly young professionals like me, had never been asked before to support the arts," Goodwin says. "It just shows what collective effort can accomplish."

Goodwin continues to serve on the CAC's Board of Trustees and is also a board member of Cincinnati Public Radio and MusicNOW, the contemporary music festival founded and directed by Bryce Dessner of rock band The National in collaboration with the Cincinnati Symphony Orchestra. The Johnson Foundation has provided funding for dozens of local arts-based projects via ArtWorks, Ensemble Theatre Cincinnati, The Mini MicroCinema, PAR Projects, and many other organizations.

—John Fox

ROBIN GUARINO

Robin Guarino has no time to bother disputing anyone's perception of opera as an out-of-touch art form in today's technology-obsessed world. She's too busy using opera to share dynamic, relevant stories with modern audiences.

Serving as the J. Ralph Corbett Distinguished Chair of Opera at the University of Cincinnati's College-Conservatory of Music (CCM) since 2007, Guarino leads a collaborative movement both within CCM and with outside organizations, particularly Cincinnati Opera, to pair state-of-the-art training with real-world experience for her students.

"My primary goals have been to support diversity, not only in our student body but in our casting and programming, and to cultivate a collaborative, compassionate and empowered environment," she says.

Her role as co-artistic director of Opera Fusion: New Works opens up opportunities for audiences and students alike. The nationally recognized partnership between Cincinnati Opera and CCM was created in 2011 to foster the development of new American operas by hosting composers and librettists to workshop story ideas with CCM students and professional artists, then present a free public performance.

A number of workshop projects have later been staged as full productions at professional opera companies, including *Fellow Travelers*, which debuted at Cincinnati Opera in 2016 and was performed by Lyric Opera of Chicago and Minnesota Opera. A recent Opera Fusion: New Works project, *Castor and Patience*, will receive its world premiere during Cincinnati Opera's 100th anniversary season in 2020.

Guarino served as stage director and dramaturg for *Blind Injustice*, a world premiere opera that enjoyed a run of sold-out performances during Cincinnati Opera's 2019 season. A collaboration with the Young Professionals Choral Collective and the Ohio Innocence Project, the work explored the true story of six people who were wrongly imprisoned and ultimately freed thanks to OIP's legal efforts.

"*Blind Injustice* was one of the most moving experiences of my life, both from a creative point of view and from an activist point of view," Guarino says. "We made work that matters and brings justice to people's lives, and I was able to have my students collaborate and co-author at the frontline. What a gift!"

Outside of her demands at CCM, Guarino has been a master teacher and artist-in-residence at the Juilliard School, San Francisco Opera Center, Wolf Trap Opera, The Glimmerglass Festival, and other prestigious young artist training programs. She became a member of the Metropolitan Opera Stage Directing Staff in 1992 and has been invited back to direct over a dozen productions. And all along the way, she connects current and former students with the opera world's biggest names and with each other.

"I'm proud of so many of my students, not only for their artistry but for their humanity and how they've chosen to live their lives as artists," Guarino says. "That's the core of my teaching: Each artist gets to be the author of his or her own life."

—John Fox

HEATHER HALLENBERG

Back in 1995, Cincinnati Shakespeare Company was an impudent startup theater called Fahrenheit. There was no Fringe Festival, no Visionaries and Voices, no Kennedy Heights Arts Center.

There were far fewer small arts organizations in our cultural ecosystem and those around were in a constant scramble for funding and capacity building.

Then along came the LeBlond-Joseph Report, which recommended that the country's first and largest united arts campaign—Cincinnati's Fine Arts Fund (FAF)—expand its investments beyond the eight organizations to which it provided operating support. It was the first tremor in a seismic shift that led to the Fund's evolution into ArtsWave.

Enter Heather Hallenberg.

Working with a shoestring budget, Hallenberg assembled an extraordinary group of volunteers who were convinced that our arts community could grow and prosper in new ways. Hallenberg knew that if the FAF added support for small and emerging organizations in addition to anchor institutions such as the Cincinnati Symphony Orchestra and Cincinnati Art Museum, the entire arts sector would advance.

The results of that conviction are all around us in our thriving arts and cultural community, rich with organizations that didn't exist in 1995. For more than 20 years, Heather Hallenberg was the best friend small arts ever had. Three words characterize her impact.

INNOVATION. Hallenberg built a chapter of Business Volunteers for the Arts (BVA) matching people with skills to similar needs in the arts community. Then she built a powerful training program, Board-Way Bound, that prepared business and community leaders to serve as directors of arts and cultural organizations. Along the way, these Cincinnati programs became best practice for the nation.

Ever the visionary, Hallenberg saw the rise of community-based arts centers and wove them together in a network that today sustains neighborhoods around the region. And she also led the charge to provide unrestricted operational funding for Cincinnati's FAF's first "associate" members— many of them are wholly part of ArtsWave's investment portfolio today.

COMMITMENT. Hallenberg's immersion in the work was unparalleled. She often rose at 4 a.m. to review resumes and prepare for interviews with potential BVAs. When a theater lost its founder and was in danger of closing, Hallenberg assembled a crisis team to work with the board and save the company, setting the stage for a brighter second act.

And Hallenberg fiercely loved her volunteers. She lavished them with genuine appreciation and support, instilling a sense of purpose and getting the best from everyone.

EXECUTION. No detail is too small, and no courtesy is forgotten, in a Hallenberg production. Like the best stage managers, Hallenberg recorded every cue and ran the show with the practice and precision that ensured a standing-O when the curtain fell. Hallenberg's two decades of service to our arts and cultural community have left their mark. Many of those small arts that she championed have grown to significant scale and undoubtable sustainability, strengthening the arts sector from within.

Best friend indeed.

—Mary Stagaman

BARBARA KELLAR

If she'd been born in a different era, Barbara Kellar thinks she may have been a criminal lawyer. But a gap in 1960s women's career options was a gain for the Cincinnati arts community, especially its Public Broadcast System (PBS) station, CET.

Kellar has spent hundreds of volunteer hours and raised millions of dollars for Cincinnati's PBS station, as well as serving many other major arts organizations over many decades.

Today, Kellar is known in Cincinnati for her tireless work running CET's Action Auction. "We worked until 2 a.m. when the auction was running," she says of herself and her army of 4,000 volunteers, mostly women. "We had to work until everything was done." She also hosts a weekly program on CET, *Showcase with Barbara Kellar*, which completed a 13th season in 2019.

Barbara and her husband, Lorrence Kellar, are known for their philanthropy in the city, particularly for their love of the arts. In fact, they met on a Cincinnati Ballet-organized trip to Russia in 1972. In 2014, they were named Philanthropists of the Year by the Association of Fundraising Professionals.

Kellar began her career in the early 1960s after earning both bachelor's and master's degrees in education from University of Cincinnati. For nine years, she taught school because "when I was growing up, teaching was the only career most of us (girls) even thought of." In 2007, she was appointed to the foundation board of trustees for her alma mater.

Among Kellar's many honors, in 1966 she was the first recipient of the Heart for the Arts award from Learning Through Art. She has also been honored as a Beacon of Light Humanitarian (2005) by Lighthouse Youth Services; by Cincinnati Ballet at its 30th Anniversary Gala for a new Lorrence T. and Barbara W. Kellar Ballet Studio; in 2010 for 40 years of service to CET and Public Television; University of Cincinnati's Award for Excellence in 2012; and by *Venue Magazine* in 2013 with a Leadership and Legacy in the Arts Award.

A past president of the Cincinnati MacDowell Society—an organization dedicated to advancing fine arts in the region—in 2019 Kellar received a MacDowell medal for her lifetime support of the arts.

What Kellar brings to her varied volunteer service roles is a strong work ethic and also business acumen. She challenges arts organizations to think more like corporations: "You have to do the math and figure out your costs when planning a fundraiser," she says. She also brings the same love of efficiency that captured her interest in time-motion studies. "I don't want to waste time. I want to do something the most efficient way possible."

A lifelong Cincinnatian, Kellar is proud of the region's strong cultural institutions. Her weekly Saturday evening TV show features guest artists discussing their lives and work. She won television's prestigious Emmy award for an episode where she rode the streetcar to highlight the innovative light installations created for the city's first BLINK event.

While she sees that her own work is valued by community leaders—the mayor gave her a key to the city—she says it also has great value for her personally. "You feel like you matter here."

—Carolyn Pione Micheli

TAMMY KERNODLE

Though she might not be a household name, Dr. Tammy L. Kernodle has impacted the music world in ways you can't imagine, solidifying her reputation as one of the leading authorities on African American music.

Kernodle was born and raised in the small city of Danville, Virginia, in 1969, and was brought up in a household with her loving parents and two younger brothers. Her father's side of the family was incredibly musically inclined. "Everyone either played the piano or sang, and some of them did multiple things," she said. Her father's mother was a bluegrass musician who played the piano, banjo and spoons, and when Kernodle turned just three years old, she began taking piano lessons from her grandmother.

Kernodle initially did not want to play the piano. But with the help from her mother, she soon developed a strong passion for playing. By the time she was nine, she knew that playing piano was part of her destiny.

Her musical taste at this young age varied, as she played everything from classical music and jazz to gospel and popular music. Her maternal great-grandmother, a direct descendent of slaves, influenced her artistic direction and focus to African-American music. "I had someone in my life who had seen almost a century's worth of change in America," she said. "That had a major impact on me and my perspective of blackness, about 'womanness,' and about the world. She relayed a lot of stories to me and my brothers about what it was like growing up in the segregated South."

A prolific singer, performer and scholar, Kernodle earned a bachelor's degree in choral music education and piano from Virginia State University before earning her master's and doctorate degrees in music

history from The Ohio State University. She has been a professor of musicology at Miami University since 1997 and has taught African-American music, gender studies in music, and 20th century American music.

In 2004, Kernodle published the book *Soul on Soul: The Life and Music of Mary Lou Williams* and, in 2011, was associate editor of the *Encyclopedia of African American Music*. She served as a consultant for the Smithsonian's National Museum of African American History and Culture's music division, working on their exhibit *Musical Crossroads*. Kernodle continues her relationship with the Smithsonian with the 2020 release of *Smithsonian Anthology of Hip-Hop and Rap*, an anthology featuring nine CDs and a 300-page book that explores the evolution of hip hop.

Kernodle was featured in the 2015 award-winning documentary *Girls in the Band*, as well as the BBC radio documentary *The Dvorak Statement* in 2017. She has also worked as a consultant with National Public Radio and The Kennedy Center for the Arts, and, from 1999–2001, served as the Scholar-in-Residence at the American Jazz Museum in Kansas City, Missouri, and helped launched their Women in Jazz Initiative.

In 2018, Kernodle received Miami University's prestigious Benjamin Harrison Medallion. She became president of the Society for American Music in 2019. She has established herself as a leading expert in African-American music, and her vast knowledge, servitude, and musical abilities make her a powerful voice in Cincinnati arts.

—Tiffany Luckey

PAM KRAVETZ

Pam Kravetz laughs recalling her art school days at the University of Cincinnati ("I was at DAA before the P," she says), where her spirit of adventure was incubated. A friend said she saw a picture of the Homecoming Queen candidates and one looked like Kravetz.

"You have a twin on campus," her friend said. "No, that's me," she responded, imitating the frozen look of horror on her friend's face. For added fun, Kravetz started wearing the Bearcat costume at UC football games. "I'll do anything once," she says.

Indeed, Kravetz has become the go-to person in Cincinnati's arts community when someone wants to do something outrageous. Lead the inaugural BLINK parade? Drive the motorized Arnold's bathtub during Bockfest? Dress up in a crazy costume for The Art of Food? Organize a synchronized swimming team at Ziegler Park? Produce and emcee fundraising events? She's your gal. "I have to find joy in life every day," Kravetz says. "I love people. I love chaos."

And yet, for almost 30 years, her day job teaching art at Harrison High School has been fairly stable and structured. Her mother was a teacher, something Kravetz never saw herself replicating, but she feels that she makes a difference in the small suburban community. "I'm super embraced there, but they don't get me," she says, pointing to her everyday wardrobe of feathers, sequins, high-top boots and chunky jewelry. "They don't understand why they support me, but they do." One of her proudest mo-

ments, Kravetz says, is when the Harrison marching band traveled to Over-the-Rhine to participate in the BLINK opening night parade in 2017 simply because she was involved.

In and around her teaching job and public appearances, Kravetz makes art at her Columbia-Tusculum home and wherever it's needed. She's shown her fiber art, ceramics, puppets, and installations at the Contemporary Arts Center, Cincinnati Art Museum, 21c Museum Hotel, The Carnegie, Kennedy Heights Arts Center and other venues, including BLINK. You might have seen her knitting handiwork at the occasional public space yarn bombings organized by her Bombshells group, or her quilts at the Ronald McDonald House and Children's Hospital.

Kravetz serves on the Board of Trustees of ArtWorks, the Art Academy of Cincinnati and The Mini Microcinema, and was named an *Enquirer* Woman of the Year in 2017. You will likely attend an arts event over the next year where she'll be the unabashed, enthusiastic emcee or greeter wearing a giant hat and a big smile—and you will be thankful that she'll do anything once.

—John Fox

QUIERA LEVY-SMITH

She's not a dancer, musician, or a painter. Yet Quiera Levy-Smith knows something good when she sees it. As a native of Chicago's South Side, she knows the fragile string that connects African-American children to the arts and how easily that line can be severed.

She also knows the benefits for her community that come from strengthening those ties. "If you're a kid in Avondale, Evanston, or West End, you might not be able to experience beauty," said Levy-Smith, who lives in Paddock Hills with her husband.

"I'm trying to be the provider (of opportunities) or to open their eyes so they can recognize beauty. Even if things are ugly, you can see beauty. But you have to have access to it. And maybe they see something they hadn't imagined. My hope is if they see a ballet dancer—and it had never occurred to them that they could be great—maybe something happens to them that they realize they can be good at something."

Levy-Smith, who has degrees in business and marketing from the University of Illinois, has put her education to good use on behalf of the arts in Cincinnati. She has worked for Playhouse in the Park and the Taft Museum of Art. And she continues to volunteer as co-chair of the Cincinnati Symphony Orchestra's Multicultural Awareness Council, serving as a liaison to link the organization with the African American and Hispanic communities. She has also

promoted groups at the Bi-Okoto Cultural Institute and Contemporary Dance Theater.

Of her many contributions to the arts community, Levy-Smith might be best known for her advocacy in dance. She stayed with an idea for five years, working to cultivate a *Black Dance is Beautiful Festival*. With support from a People's Liberty Project Grant, her idea to promote black choreographers and dancers came to fruition in 2015.

"My talent is finding the people with the talent and finding platforms for them," she said. Yet Levy-Smith doesn't promote black artists just because they are African American. "I support really great theater. I support really great art. I really support really great dance involving people who look like me."

So it has been with the *Black Dance is Beautiful Festival*. Her latest project is forming a dance company under that name that combines local African dance, black ballet, and hip hop dance groups. "It's a way I can make a difference," Levy-Smith said. "I want people to see what I see. There is a lot of beauty here."

—Mark Curnutte

RHODA MAYERSON

Rhoda Mayerson's impact on the arts in Cincinnati is immeasurable. Every one of Cincinnati's major arts organizations, as well as the School for Creative and Performing Arts (SCPA), has benefited from generous gifts from the Mayerson Family Foundation.

Rhoda Mayerson's husband, Manuel, who died in 2012, also loved the arts. Together they helped make Cincinnati a world-class arts destination rivaled by few U.S. cities, large or small.

But the Mayersons' gifts to the arts in Cincinnati went well beyond monetary contributions. Their son, Dr. Neal Mayerson of Cincinnati, who is president of the Manuel D. and Rhoda Mayerson Foundation, said his parents "always felt they had a lot more to contribute than a check. Somehow they found the time and the energy to sit on a lot of boards, go to a lot of performances—and still raise kids and build a successful business." (Neal has a sister and a brother.)

Mayerson has served on the boards of most of the city's large arts organizations, and as she reflected back on her life of dedication to the arts, it was the time given to those boards that she considers her greatest contribution. She also served on the board of the Boca Raton, Florida, Museum of Art.

But, she says, it wasn't always a matter of pleasure. It was hard work. She remembered countless drives to board meetings from her home in Amberley Village, passing a golf course and wondering, "Why aren't I out there enjoying myself?" But it always was clear that this work fit her values and offered greater meaning.

She always enjoyed the aesthetic more than the athletic. Early in her adult life, she began to assemble a collection of world-class contemporary works that now comprise the Mayerson Foundation Art Gallery in the Scripps Center in downtown Cincinnati.

As a patron and collector, Mayerson had a significant impact on the permanent collection of the Cincinnati Art Museum. As a trustee, she served on the Art Acquisitions Committee during each of her terms and brought her knowledge and passion for enjoying and acquiring artwork to that committee's work. The Mayersons also established two contemporary art galleries in the Cincinnati Art Museum.

Mayerson did as much as she could to pass on her love for the arts to young people. Among the many places one finds the Mayerson name directly connected to the arts are the Mayerson Artistic Excellence Program at the School for Creative and Performing Arts, which brings prominent artists in several fields to SCPA to perform and interact with students, and SCPA's Corbett Mayerson Scholarship Award.

The Mayersons' participation and contributions to the arts extended beyond Cincinnati. Mayerson has been a frequent producer of Broadway and traveling Broadway productions. A partial list includes: *The Wedding Singer*, 2006, producer; *Jersey Boys*, 2005, associate producer; *Little Shop of Horrors*, 2003, associate producer; *Hairspray*, 2003, associate producer; and *The Producers*, 2001, associate producer.

How can Cincinnati possibly repay Rhoda Mayerson for her support and love for the arts?

During an interview at her home in August 2019, she had an answer: "Go out and buy some tickets."

—Dave Caudill

DR. CAROLYN L. MAZLOOMI

Dr. Carolyn L. Mazloomi has been a full-time artist for over 30 years. A self-taught quilter, curator of multiple traveling exhibitions, retired aerospace engineer, and award winning author, the 72-year old founded the Women of Color Quilters Network in 1985.

Mazloomi says, "There needed to be an organization to inform quilt artists about the historical significance of their work: how their work is important to the culture—as well as inform them of the monetary value of their work."

Some 35 years later, the quilting organization has more than 1,700 members who Mazloomi assists through exhibition organizing, technical development, grant writing, and other services the organization manages.

For the past 15 years, Mazloomi has devoted more time to curating exhibitions for museums in the Ohio Valley region that tackle difficult subject matter: issues such as racism, women's rights, and Black Lives Matter. "I bring these topics to the public in hopes of eliminating some of the negativity, misinformation and hate associated with them," Mazloomi writes via email.

And if there is a common thread in the many roles that the artist has played, advocating for women—particularly those in at-risk populations such as women of color, immigrants, the elderly, and children—is at the heart of everything Dr. Mazloomi does.

Though she had long admired quilts, Mazloomi says she didn't realize she had any artistic creativity herself until she made her first one 45 years ago. The artist explains, "I taught myself. I read a book and just tried to get through it," she remembers laughingly. "I didn't realize I could make art until I attempted it."

"All of us are artists," Mazloomi adds thoughtfully, without skipping a beat. "We just have to make that attempt." And so this Jane-of-all-trades began experimenting with fabrics to tell stories in a narrative folk tradition—all the while seeking to uplift her fellow artists.

With both artistic pursuits as well as leadership roles, Mazloomi embodies her mantra that "art has the capacity to touch the spirit, engage, educate, and heal in ways that words alone cannot."

Among her various honors, Mazloomi has authored 11 books on quilting; met with and made work for civil rights leader and U.S. Congressman from Georgia, John Lewis; and presented one of her quilts to former President of South Africa, Nelson Mandela, at the 13th International AIDS Conference in Durban, South Africa. Mazloomi was awarded the Black Caucus of the American Library Association Literary Award for Best Nonfiction Book in 1999, and the first Ohio Heritage Fellowship Award in 2003 for *Spirits of the Cloth: Contemporary African American Quilts*. She was named National Heritage Fellow in 2014 by the National Endowment for the Arts.

"Being involved in the arts has given me wonderful experiences. I've met such great women who mean so much to me, and I've learned so many life lessons from the women I've worked with—and all of them have given me joy," she testifies. "I don't think many people can say that about their work."

—Maria Seda-Reeder

CONSTANCE McCLURE

For Constance McClure, art education is never truly finished. "I'm still learning," said the artist and professor emerita at the Art Academy of Cincinnati (AAC). After nearly five decades of teaching, she remains as much a student as are her students.

"I tell them, 'I'm learning stuff from you as you're doing it. You're my experiments.'"

As a child in Huntington, West Virginia, during the Great Depression, McClure's artistic side was encouraged by her mother. "I was a Depression-era baby, but we always had books," McClure said. "And I used to draw on the empty page in the front and she'd let me. But paper was a premium. I'd used lined tablet paper, anything I could get my hands on I would draw. All you need's a pencil."

Her mother enrolled her in the Ringling School of Art in Sarasota, Florida, where she married classmate Robert McNesky and started a family. While her husband became a sculptor and teacher at the University of Cincinnati's College of Design, Architecture and Art, as a young mother in the mid-twentieth century, she was expected to stay home, not attend art school.

"I thought, 'I want to go back and get my degree. I want to teach. And I want to do my art. I want to be known as me,'" she said. "And that's when I started using my name, McClure. Instead of Connie McClure McNesky, it was Constance McClure."

She taught drawing classes at the College of Mount St. Joseph (now University) while taking courses herself and graduated with a bachelor's degree in art in 1971. Art Academy faculty member Tony Batchelor gave her a figure-drawing class to teach at the Academy in 1974, and she has been teaching there ever since.

As an artist and teacher, McClure has sought to learn new techniques, sometimes teaching herself, and then incorporating them into her classroom. In her materials and techniques class at AAC, she instructed on metalpoint, egg tempera, hand-ground oil paints, encaustic, and frescoes.

She was awarded a grant to study for a summer at Skowhegan School of Painting and Sculpture in Madison, Maine, to learn the ancient technique of making frescos, which are wall paintings on wet lime plaster. It's one of the most challenging mediums for students to tackle. "It's a rigorous, rigorous medium," McClure said. "But when you do one, by golly, you feel like you've really accomplished something. Especially if it's realism."

McClure's own work is grounded in realism, mostly human figures in everyday life. She has a silverpoint portrait of Thomas Satterwhite Noble hanging in the AAC's campus building in Over-The-Rhine, and 22 pieces in the collection of the Cincinnati Art Museum.

And generations of students to learn from.

—Jeff Suess

MARY McCULLOUGH-HUDSON

Mary McCullough-Hudson had a plan. She was going to be an opera singer. Step one was to graduate from the College-Conservatory of Music (CCM) with bachelor's and master's degrees in music.

While step two included singing with the Cincinnati Opera, she says now that "an opera star was not being born!"

But a relationship with Greg Hudson, whom she would marry in 1980, was blossoming. They met doing community theater and briefly gave the Big Apple a try. Ultimately deciding that New York was not for them, Mary and Greg planted deep roots in Cincinnati.

As Mary started her job search, she learned of a position at the Fine Arts Fund (FAF) as secretary to Paul Sittenfeld, then director of the annual fundraising campaign. Although she had no administrative experience, McCullough-Hudson reports that "Paul had a gut feeling that I could add value to the organization—and he needed to get through the campaign!"

After the campaign, McCullough-Hudson was promoted several times, including campaign director in 1984, a leadership role she played for a decade. It's easy to see that it was destiny for McCullough-Hudson to become executive director in 1994 when Erv Oberschmitt retired. Fast forward two decades, McCullough-Hudson retired in 2014.

By the time McCullough-Hudson joined the FAF in 1979, the organization had just passed its mid-century mark. The Cincinnati Institute of Fine Arts (its original name) was founded in 1927 by Charles P. and Anna Sinton Taft who gave a $1 million endowment matched by $2.5 million from community donors. It wasn't until 1949, however, that the first community-wide campaign in the nation was launched in Cincinnati. It was branded as the Fine Arts Fund and supported four organizations.

Thirty years later, when McCullough-Hudson joined the FAF, the campaign was generating $2.5 million, mostly from workplace giving campaigns insti-tuted in 1973. When she retired in 2014, the campaign had grown to over $12 million, the largest campaign of its kind in the United States. The number of participating arts organizations had grown to over 100!

Across McCullough-Hudson's 35-year career, there was much change and many accomplishments, including a major undertaking to shift how the community thinks and talks about the arts.

In 2008, the FAF commissioned a study to compare its contributor list to patrons of Cincinnati's largest arts organizations. The result: "Nearly 80% of the fund's donors had zero engagement with…the symphony…or the museum." What contributors wanted is civic health, which equated to a vibrant arts scene.

Despite some initial trepidation about making waves, McCullough-Hudson relied on proof repeated over a century's time that the Fine Arts Fund could withstand changing times. Today, she says "I am most proud of getting ahead of the curve in responding to market realities. While it was clear to us (at the FAF) that the wheels could come off, that sense of urgency wasn't apparent to everyone."

Continued relevance felt worth the risk that accompanied a change in mission, name, and focus on the creative energy of the entire region. In September 2010, the FAF unveiled its new name, ArtsWave, meant to evoke the ripple effect that arts can have on a region. McCullough-Hudson spent her remaining years as CEO making sure that the trinity of mission, innovation, and sustainability was balanced and leading toward an even stronger and more inclusive organization.

Recognition for her work can be measured in many ways, including receiving CCM's distinguished alumna award.

—Kathy Merchant

ELLEN MUSE-LINDEMAN

She works in a big beautiful house, a 19th-century classic and she lives so close to it that she can walk there. She loves what she does. Her name, Ellen Muse-Lindeman, has a poetic ring.

As executive director of the Kennedy Heights Arts Center, she has played an instrumental role in the rejuvenation of its neighborhood and helped to ensure that the stellar, white wood-frame house on Montgomery Road prospers and helps its community to thrive.

The big house serves as more than an arts center. It could be called an energy generator. Not only do Muse-Lindeman and her staff promote and exhibit the arts, they sponsor arts education in schools, a summer arts camp for almost 300 kids on a pay-as-you-can basis, concerts in the center's Lindner Annex, and they do all this and more in what she calls a "spirit of inclusion."

Muse-Lindeman sees the arts center as a great example of the power of the arts to bring people together. "We're all about leveraging that power," she said.

Muse-Lindeman came to the center 11 years ago after working for 15 years in leadership roles at Covington's Center for Great Neighborhoods, where she also promoted arts and culture to help invigorate declining neighborhoods. She brought the skills honed in Covington to Kennedy Heights, and as she injected energy and channeled resources into the arts center, the neighborhood experienced a concurrent upswing.

Muse-Lindeman points with pride to Kennedy Heights' ongoing commercial transformation. She credits the arts center's Lindner Annex as a catalyst. A donation from the Lindner family helped turn a long-vacant former Kroger into a space that houses performance and meeting rooms, a digital media classroom, artists' studios, and a woodworking shop.

Mary Kidd Ray, a founding board member of the arts center, says Muse-Lindeman has been a champion of the arts center movement throughout Cincinnati. When Muse-Lindeman arrived at the arts center a little more than a decade ago, Ray said, "something magical began to happen."

The center got its start in 2004 when a group of like-minded and generous volunteers bought the Kennedy house and established it as a nonprofit. "We did teach art and had exhibitions," Ray says, but Muse-Lindeman took the center to another level. "Suddenly the neighborhood was changing, and Ellen changed us. She changed me. She has cast a positive glow over the whole neighborhood."

Bill Lennard, the arts center's board president, says Muse-Lindeman has been the "anchor of an increasingly vibrant, creative and inclusive community."

Her interest in the arts found early expression as Muse-Lindeman studied theater at Ohio's College of Wooster. She went on to a master's program in social work administration at the University of Cincinnati.

She says she's grateful for the recognition her own work in the arts has received, but she hopes for equal recognition for the Kennedy Heights Arts Center and for the strides Covington continues to make toward artistic and cultural vitality.

She also likes to turn the spotlight on the people she's been fortunate to work with. About them, she says, "I've been blessed."

—Dave Caudill

JEAUNITA ÌFẸ́WÁNDÉ CHÂTEAU WEATHERSBY OLÓWÈ

The life of Jeaunita Ìfẹ́wándé Château Weathersby Olówè has at times been as lilting as her name, moving gracefully across the years. Yet, in other intervals, it has been filled with unexpected twists and turns befitting her vocation as a dancer and arts educator.

The latest moves, hard and unplanned, hit her in 2018. A diagnosis revealed breast cancer, and her two-decade professional partnership in the Bi-Oko-to Drum & Dance Theatre and Cultural Institute and marriage to Adebola Olówè both came to an end. Still, true to her upbringing in the 1970s and '80s on Over-The-Rhine's Republic Street, well before its gentrification, Jeaunita Olówè wouldn't stop. "My parents always said, 'Just because you grew up in the ghetto doesn't mean you're from the ghetto,'" she said.

Olówè has formed Ìfẹ́wándé Cultural Programs, her single-woman multi-cultural dance, arts education, and integration consulting business. As 2019 turned to 2020, her triple negative breast cancer was in a good place that left her with the energy to teach several hundred students in "arts and culture" schools each week as Cincinnati Public Schools' resident artist.

She made a concession to cut back on her schedule. "The defining moment was when I learned that I couldn't be there for everyone else if I wasn't here for me," she said. "I couldn't do the world. I had to do me."

Yet this is a woman who has done the world, having performed and taught dance in her ex-husband's native Nigeria, several other African nations, and throughout Europe on two U.S. military and NATO tours. She also worked as an instructor for the Kentucky Arts Council and Kentucky Department of Education in its African core content. Those were the times she has flown high. Then came all of the hard knocks.

Nothing new for the girl from Republic Street: as a sophomore on academic scholarship as a math and statistics major at Miami University, Olówè was called home by her mother to help care for an 18-month-old niece who'd been abandoned. When one door closes, another opens. Leaving school led to a series of jobs at Cincinnati Ballet under the tutelage of Kathy DeLaura, the ballet's former executive director. "I remember telling Kathy, 'We need more brown girls to dance. We need to make it less difficult for brown girls to dance,'" Olówè said. Her work as the first African-American administrator at the Ballet improved access for minority children through enduring youth programs that include the *Pirouette Club* and *CincyDance!*

"My whole life would have been different if I'd stayed at Miami," Olówè said while in a restaurant eating breakfast on a December morning. Her shirt says it all: *Live Your Truth*. Speaking with conviction and the type of passion reserved for people who've looked their mortality in the eye at close range: "I believe so whole-heartedly in what I do with the children I teach. I am doing what I am supposed to be doing. It's my purpose. I'm not here to turn you into a drummer, I'm not here to turn you into a dancer. I want you to walk away with one thing, one great thing, a great moment in your young life, an experience you will carry with you for the rest of your days."

—Mark Curnutte

MELODY SAWYER RICHARDSON

If there are two things Melody Sawyer Richardson loves, it's the arts and helping people. That she has forged a successful philanthropic career at the intersection of both should come as no surprise.

A Cincinnati native, Richardson graduated from Seven Hills Academy before attending Denison University, later graduating from the University of Cincinnati with a degree in social work. She spent several years in that field, even crossing paths with famed anthropologist Margaret Mead. After moving to New York City, Richardson decided to go to business school to get her MBA. And then she decided to apply to law school, too. She got in, graduating in four years with both degrees.

Richardson embarked on a career on Wall Street as an attorney, and then at Chase Bank, before moving back to Cincinnati in 1994 and into her family home, River High, in Hyde Park. She worked tirelessly at renovating the estate, which became a central gathering point for many denizens of Cincinnati's arts crowd. She threw herself headlong into all the cultural experiences Cincinnati had to offer, getting season tickets to many organizations, including the May Festival and Cincinnati Symphony Orchestra.

Richardson loves Cincinnati. Anything she could do to help it, she did. Join the team behind the opening of the Aronoff Center for the Arts in 1996 as general counsel and vice president of community

relations? Check. Serve as the chairman of the board for the Cincinnati Symphony Orchestra (the second woman to hold that position) during the tenuous economic downturn in 2008, building the board back up member by member until she left in 2014? Check. Serve as the chairman of the board for Cincinnati Ballet? Check. Champion the Big Pig Gig in 2000, a public art installation undertaken by ArtWorks? Check. Richardson was and is tenacious and persistent in her approach to Cincinnati's arts, always with the end-goal in sight of making the community a better place.

Currently, Richardson splits her time between New York City and Cincinnati. She has served on numerous other boards, including Cincinnati Opera, the National Underground Railroad Freedom Center, and the Ohio Humanities Council, and is involved with the Cincinnati chapter of the National Society of Colonial Dames of America. She has left an indelible mark on the Greater Cincinnati arts community, and the community at large. Her leadership, drive and passion are priceless contributions in the city's illustrious philanthropic lineage, where, years from now, her name will stand out among the rest.

—Leyla Shokoohe

ANNIE RUTH

Like a 1970s Black Arts Movement throwback, Annie Ruth swaths herself in multi-hued, ankle-length African textiles. Sometimes likewise wrapping her head, she wears open sandals in warm weather.

She may be adorned for another time and place, but she is present in the here and now.

Annie Ruth is known as a poet and a largely self-taught illustrator; however, those unfamiliar with her work in those disciplines may certainly know her for Dada Rafiki: The Women Gather. It's her annual celebration of community stakeholders—the black folks mostly unnoticed and unheralded but who nevertheless do and have changed lives—co-presented with the Cincinnati Arts Association.

In the Kiswahili dialect of East Africa Dada Rafiki means "sister friend." It honored 26 women its first year and will celebrate 15 years in 2020.

Annie Ruth describes Dada Rafiki as "a way of saying, 'I see you sister,' to encourage women to keep doing what they're doing. It's not an award. It's who God placed on my heart. It's a way to love on sisters."

Folded into this homegrown pageantry is a pinch of social justice, a dash of racism beat down, and a heap of philanthropy.

To counter the negative press of the then-new Community Action Agency of Hamilton County complex under the leadership of a black woman and located in predominately black Bond Hill, Annie Ruth decided to hold Dada Rafiki at that site the first year.

In doing so, she rested on the tent poles she knew would work to hold aloft her lofty goals. "As a poet and a visual artist, you can tackle those sensitive subjects without hitting people over the head."

The mother of two adult children and grandmother of six keeps her artistic energy fueled by hosting First Thursdays, her free monthly open-studio workshop in the bright studio-turned-classroom on the second floor of New Prospect Baptist Church in Bond Hill.

Poets, visual artists and makers of all skill levels are welcome.

Annie Ruth knows what she provides is a speedy remedy for what ails communities of color. Art making can be a quick Band-Aid which, left unattended, could leave the minor cuts of countless social –isms to fester into life-altering failures. "It is community members who provide what is needed instantly."

Annie Ruth says Cincinnati could use more of what she and others do who use art as a healer. But for now, and for Annie Ruth, there's a balm in Bond Hill that can be spread. "Even though art is this vehicle that can tear down walls, there are still these racial barriers, socioeconomic barriers, within the art world. The problem we have in Cincinnati is getting people within the room to experience (it).

"I want my legacy to be that I used my art to build bridges…and I used my art to empower people."

Annie Ruth has published more than 30 curriculum sets with accompanying children's books. In 2020, she will hold her fifth annual girls' conference during which former Dada Rafiki honorees will mentor girls chosen from throughout Cincinnati. One hundred girls age 13–19 will be honored and will be mentored throughout the following year.

The beat goes on.

—Kathy Y. Wilson

ANN SANTEN

Ann Santen raised her children in Cincinnati, brought classical music to our homes, served on boards, volunteered at the Cincinnati Nature Center, earned her degree here, and chaired the search for the head of the Cincinnati Symphony Orchestra, Louis Langrée.

These are the life accomplishments of the great and the good. But they fail to tell the complete story of this singular woman.

To know Santen, you need to realize that she started as a volunteer at WGCU before working her way up to Music Director, then General Manager. That she earned her college degree after having three children and going to the University of Cincinnati at age 38. That one of her greatest accomplishments came not in a board room, but in the brutal sun of an archeological dig in southwest Greece where Santen was part of a team that made one of the great discoveries of the past 50 years.

Smithsonian Magazine put the significant find in perspective: "The Pylos grave, with its wealth of undisturbed burial objects and, at its bottom, a largely intact skeleton, offers a nearly unprecedented window into this time (3,500 years ago)—and what it reveals is calling into question our most basic ideas about the roots of Western civilization."

Santen's path to that gravesite explains a lot about her. In the late 1990s, Santen stepped down from WGCU, and her husband Harry started talking about retirement. With the kids grown, the Santens went to France for a year.

After returning, Santen thought she would like to study French at the University of Cincinnati. It was not long, however, before she realized she was most interested in archeology. Because she does nothing in half measure, Santen started going on digs around the world. This is the work that separates dabblers and dilettantes from those with real commitment. "Digging is the hardest physical work I have ever done. And the hottest and the filthiest," Santen says with a smile.

She went on digs for 15 years in a row and turned 80 in Pylos making the discovery of a lifetime. "It was extraordinarily important," Santen said. "It was my trench, I was digging. It really was a 'wow.'" There were not many digs after that. The trenches are getting too deep, the ground too hard.

Santen had already found another way to contribute to the arts and her city—two things she loves very much. It is music, particularly the Cincinnati Symphony Orchestra, that ties everything together. "It is the central musical organization in the city. The musicians teach across the city, they perform in other ensembles."

Santen's time as Music Director at WGCU helped her realize that she did not want to just appreciate and study music, she wanted to help bring more music into the world. She understood that much of the classical music we enjoy now is the result of brilliant musicians from centuries ago and the largess of sponsors who allowed that music to happen.

So Ann and Harry now bring new music into the world, commissioning new works by current artists. "Commissioning new music is my passion. We have commissioned over 30 pieces," Santen said. "There has to be new music coming in for it to stay alive."

This is Santen's way to bring joy to people today, and possibly centuries from now.

—John Faherty

ROSEMARY SCHLACHTER

Rosemary Schlachter is the epitome of generosity, serving as both philanthropic leader and pillar of the Cincinnati community since the 1960s. A natural-born leader and Cincinnati native, she is the owner of 25th Hour, a highly successful fundraising firm.

She truly lives her belief that giving back "is a way of life" and serves on numerous boards, including past board and executive committee member at the Cincinnati Symphony Orchestra and Emeritus Board member at Cincinnati Ballet. Schlachter sees her role as an enabler of the arts through philanthropy, and enjoys the privilege of being an audience member who truly appreciates the artistic spiritual connection.

From selling girl scout cookies to organizing prom, Schlachter's drive to make things happen started as a young girl. Her love of art also manifested early with ballet classes, a wonderful drama teacher, and a pivotal moment in high school when Marie Speziale, former associate principal trumpet of the Cincinnati Symphony Orchestra, played for her high school.

After attending Edgecliff College (now part of Xavier University) where she studied and taught English, in 1980 she was recruited by arts advocate and patron, Irma Lazarus, to revitalize Young Friends of the Arts (YFA), a unique organization focused on developing young audiences for Cincinnati arts. Schlachter fostered the transition of YFA into Enjoy the Arts, which continued to thrive for almost 30 years as it laid the foundation for today's programs focused on engaging young professionals.

The decision to lead YFA changed Schlachter's life, training her in arts management and public relations, and ultimately paving the path to her successful firm. She also met her husband Mark, an artist focused on large metal sculptures and photography, at a YFA event. Their four successful children carry on the legacy of art in their own careers. But it was Schlachter's relationship with Louise Nippert, also an arts advocate and patron, that helped accelerate her career. Mrs. Nippert provided invaluable mentorship, instilling confidence that resulted in Schlachter being named an *Enquirer* Woman of the Year in 1993.

In a lifetime filled with a tradition of leadership and giving back, Schlachter has many experiences to share, but two highlights hold a special place in her heart.

As current (2019) Board President of the Contemporary Arts Center, Schlachter's work was proclaimed to be "way cool" by her son, and she loved being on the board of the Cincinnati Shakespeare Company to help foster high-quality productions. As a professional fundraiser, she teaches philanthropy. In doing so, Rosemary joins a legion of extraordinary women who have dedicated their lives to generosity and creating an art-filled world that fuels spirituality for us all.

—Christi Geary

KRISTEN SCHLOTMAN

Stop to think about the breadth of Cincinnati's vibrant arts and culture scene, stretching from dance to visual art to music and beyond. If your mind leaps to include film, you can thank Kristen Schlotman.

Schlotman is in her 23rd year as executive director for Film Cincinnati, a nonprofit organization founded in 1987 as the Greater Cincinnati and Northern Kentucky Film Commission. Film Cincinnati attracts, promotes, and cultivates film, television, and commercial production throughout the region.

Film Cincinnati is also, in Schlotman's words, "a one-stop shop for everything film-making, from script to screen." The films *Carol*, *Ides of March*, *Traffic*, *Seabiscuit*, *Elizabethtown*, and *The Public* represent only a handful of the major films that Schlotman and Film Cincinnati have lured to the area. Schlotman is proud to point out that every single producer has come back to Cincinnati for another project!

When Film Cincinnati was still a fledgling operation, Schlotman says they talked about film as an art form and to build awareness of film as an industry and job creator. "I spent the first ten years talking about how this was an opportunity for our city," she says. "You have to have the tenacity and willingness for the long haul to make impact. Nothing really happens overnight."

At the time, film studios were taking their business to affordable cities in states offering tax incentives, an idea that Schlotman advocated for based on its potential to stimulate economic growth. "We were pioneers for Ohio," Schlotman says, sharing credit with the Greater Cleveland Film Commission.

Schlotman considers the resulting Ohio Motion Picture Tax Credit to be the crowning achievement of her career. The credit began in 2011 at $20 million over two years. Ohio's film commissions demonstrated $40 million in related economic impact. The tax credit has since doubled twice, now $40 million a year.

"That was (the moment) when we were able to garner enough work to show people that they could ultimately have a full-time job in this industry, right here in Ohio," Schlotman explains. "People were starting to join the union or graduate from film school and want to stay in Cincinnati."

Film Cincinnati drives economic impact for the state, but the organization itself has operated as a nonprofit since 1991—the first such film commission worldwide to be structured as a 501(c)(3), though many have since adopted similar models. Schlotman and her team write grants, work with corporations, and seek out partners who believe in community vitality and economic development.

"When there are movie stars in town, people assume they pay us. People assume we're a company of 30 people," she laughs. "We are a nonprofit that is always looking for new and innovative ways to raise money because we believe this organization makes our community a better place to live and work."

Ultimately her work has always come down to more than money for Schlotman. "It's a constant struggle, because you dance between arts and culture vs. economic development," she muses. "But the arts and culture piece is really important to me. We have such a rich history in Cincinnati—with the symphony, opera, classic arts organizations—and suddenly, in the last few years, people are talking about film."

"When I was 23 and just starting out, I wondered, 'Why isn't anybody talking about film, and why aren't there opportunities for someone like me?'" She pauses. "It's part of our fabric of arts and culture now."

—Erica Reid

REBECCA "REBA" SENSKE

Reba Senske came at costume design from a sideways direction. She had long known how to sew, making things and creating patterns. But when it came time to choose a major in college, she went with fine art.

Then one summer, while attending Southern Illinois University, Senske found a costume design class in a class catalog. And then she found out there was a summer season of theater she could get involved with immediately. And then she discovered that there was an extra tuition remission opportunity for which she qualified. And she's been designing costumes ever since!

Senske landed in Cincinnati through a stroke of precociousness: while working in a small theater in Memphis, as the often-only pair of hands for the costume shop, she sent letters of inquiry to theaters throughout the country with larger budgets. Playhouse in the Park eventually got back to her at the end of the summer in 1979.

Now the associate costume designer at the University of Cincinnati's College-Conservatory of Music (CCM), Senske previously served as the associate costume designer for Playhouse in the Park for ten years, from 1979 to 1989. She works occasionally with the Ensemble Theatre Cincinnati and Cincinnati Opera, too.

Senske's forty years of experience mean that she's particularly adept at maneuvering relationships with the people who are in her costumes as well as the people who commission them. She's learned to listen when an actor says his or her neck disappears in certain cuts, or when a dancer requests something they can feel at their waist.

Big musical numbers at CCM, the types of shows Senske is most prone to do these days, require less hyper-focused attention to detail and more a general wash of things. They are more like a watercolor used to set up the story's big picture. In contrast, straight dramas tend to be more like a television series or a movie, where the smallest details are important and meaningful. Solving the puzzle of what is needed to best tell the story is one of Senske's favorite challenges.

The variety of work in her portfolio is what she views as her legacy. From small, intense dramas like *True West* and *Buried Child*; to classics like *Alice in Wonderland, The Turn of the Screw* and *Calisto*; to ballets like *King Arthur's Camelot* and contemporary works like *Legally Blonde*—variety is what keeps Senske doing what she does.

How lucky for Cincinnati.

—Leyla Shokoohe

MARIE SPEZIALE

From a young age, Marie Speziale knew exactly what she wanted—to be a trumpeter. Growing up in Tampa, Florida, as a second-generation Italian immigrant, there was always music in her home.

"When my parents moved from New York to Tampa, my dad became enamored of the Afro-Cuban music that we know now as Salsa," she said, adding that he taught himself to play piano and, with his friends, formed a band. It was there, in her living room as they rehearsed, that she first heard a trumpet live.

She would go on to become the first woman trumpeter in a major symphony orchestra, an accolade she achieved serving as the Cincinnati Symphony Orchestra's (CSO) associate principal trumpet for 32 years, from 1964 until retirement in 1996.

On what initially drew her to the instrument, Speziale describes its sound as brilliant and exciting. "The other thing, too, is back in those days, the band director and other people were saying 'little girls don't play the trumpet.' (They would) give us flutes, clarinets, saxophone, maybe. I kept saying, 'Oh no.' However small those little footprints were, I stood my ground."

A graduate of the University of Cincinnati's College-Conservatory of Music (CCM), she was first invited to play with the CSO as a soloist in her sophomore year. She would go on to play with them several times before joining CSO as associate principal trumpet. She played with an array of orchestras for local organizations including Cincinnati Ballet, Cincinnati May Festival, Cincinnati Pops, and Cincinnati Opera.

In the mid-1960s, she notably performed in a concert alongside legendary jazz musician Duke El-lington, one of the first crossovers between jazz and a major symphony orchestra. She fondly recalls that Ellington, near the concert's tail-end, invited her and a clarinetist to come on stage and play a few jazz tunes and ballads with him. Other performance highlights include playing alongside Dave Brubeck on NBC's *The Tonight Show Starring Johnny Carson* and multiple European and world tours, including a 10-week tour playing at military bases during the Vietnam War, which she calls some of the most emotional moments of her entire career.

A Professor Emerita of Trumpet at the Shepard School of Music at Rice University, she conducted the Rice Brass Choir and has performed with the Houston Grand Opera, Houston Symphony Orchestra, Houston Ballet, and Houston Pops. (Speziale also previously taught at CCM and Indiana University.)

In the span of her career, her achievements have been great, including recording soundtracks for James Brown in his early years at King Records and, in 1999, attending the Tokyo International Music Festival as one of only six Americans (and the only woman) to perform in its Super World Orchestra.

Post-retirement, she is now living back in Cincinnati, where she was inducted into the city's Jazz Hall of Fame in 2017. "In many ways, I feel so blessed," she said. "There was no way for me to imagine the kind of career that I've had."

—Mackenzie Manley

MARY STAGAMAN

It was a production of George Bernard Shaw's *Saint Joan* at the Cincinnati Playhouse that sparked Mary Stagaman's commitment to the arts. "I was in high school, and this was the first drama I had seen on stage," she recalled.

"In those three hours, my passion was formed. The arts have been woven throughout my career and are part and parcel of my life."

Stagaman put her passion to work at the Playhouse, beginning as a volunteer usher and moving into paid roles on the administrative staff. Later, while pursuing a successful avocation as a freelance writer, she profiled artists for *Cincinnati Magazine* and WGUC's member magazine, *Artscape*. For 12 years, while working at the University of Cincinnati (UC), she mentored master's candidates in arts administration from CCM.

Today, Stagaman is Vice President, Inclusion at the Cincinnati USA Regional Chamber, where she is the architect of Diverse by Design, an initiative to attract and retain diverse talent and make our region more welcoming for all.

But it's as a volunteer that Stagaman has made the greatest impact on the Cincinnati arts community.

While running Fine Arts Fund (FAF) workplace campaigns as an administrator at UC in the 1990s, she was tapped to join the nascent Arts Services Office's Advisory Committee. The office was an outgrowth of the LeBlond-Joseph Report, which recommended that the FAF expand its support beyond the "big eight" arts groups it had traditionally funded.

Working alongside Heather Hallenberg, director of the office, Stagaman helped shape a chapter of Business Volunteers for the Arts and a board-member training program, Boardway Bound. That work led to an invitation to join the FAF Board of Directors, providing a broader platform for Stagaman's persistent voice to grow support for smaller arts organizations.

Stagaman advocated for providing much-needed operating funding for emerging organizations such as Ensemble Theatre Cincinnati, Cincinnati Shakespeare Company, the Kennedy Heights and Clifton Community Arts Centers, and many more. This led to the creation of a new funding category and additional seats on the FAF board.

But it was the Fund's decision to realign its mission in 2010 that transformed the organization from a funder to a partner in sustaining and growing the arts sector.

"There was a lot of discussion about whether this was the right move," Stagaman said. "I facilitated the discussion at the board meeting when the vote took place. It was nerve-racking and exhilarating at the same time." Ultimately, the board voted in favor of remaking the organization for the future, and ArtsWave was born, as was the Blueprint for Collective Action which Stagaman helped shape.

In 2019, 44 organizations received sustaining operating support from ArtsWave, and some 80 more received project support, fulfilling the promise of that bold move by the FAF board.

Stagaman, now one of only five women designated a Life Trustee for ArtsWave, could call that a legacy. But there's more to come.

Marrying her work in inclusion for the Cincinnati Chamber with her commitment to the arts, she is co-chair for Flow, a series of performances featuring world-class African American artists who elevate and celebrate Black culture.

"I have a deep belief that the arts have power to transcend the everyday, to bring us together across many things that divide us—like culture, background, income—better than anything else," Stagaman said. "We need to present art that reflects and represents our entire community and bring the community together to experience it. Flow is another step along the way."

—Ray Cooklis

TOILYNN O'NEAL TURNER

Because of her legendary father's sacrifice for his love of art, Toilynn O'Neal Turner knows precisely what she'll call her memoir when the time comes: *Fig Newtons and Fried Bologna.*

When she traveled, Turner's mother left money for food. But Robert O'Neal, the late visionary founder of Cincinnati Arts Consortium who died unexpectedly December 20, 2018, skimped on food and instead used the money for art, convincing his kids they were eating fruits and vegetables when they ate Fig Newtons. "He definitely lived that frugal artist's life."

Despite—or perhaps because of—those early hardships, Turner grew up living firsthand an artful and art-filled life. "It's a legacy pass. He never pushed me. He always (planted) those seeds" she says of her father.

Indeed. Robert O'Neal founded the Arts Consortium February, 1972; Turner was born September 1972.

She got D's studying zoology at The Ohio State University and begrudgingly took art classes to bolster her grades. At the tender age of 21, Turner took over the helm of the Arts Consortium during its transition from its original Linn Street home in the West End to its final resting place in Union Terminal. She led the Consortium from 1993–2006.

Turner learned during her tenure as director and curator what many heads of black arts institutions in America know: small but mighty, they cannot exist for art's sake alone. These organizations are Swiss Army knives. "We thought we were accountable for every aspect of the black community. We (also) had to be a social service agency."

That experience as a leader utilizing art as a tool for social justice and inclusion radiates throughout her present work. "Everything I do ties into art. Art is a good tool to deal with edgy topics. I learned more from (the Arts Consortium) than I did in college. It was such a humongous village for me to learn from."

That village comprises a rarified roll call of Cincinnati black artists: Gilbert Young, Velma Morris, Terrence Corbin, Thom Phelps, the NeoAncestralists, Liz Pressley-Fields and Joyce Young. Further, stellar internationally known artists like sculptor and lithographer Elizabeth Catlett were exhibited.

All told, the proximity to that art and to those artists imbued Turner with a hard-won expertise called upon across this city.

A graduate of St. Ursula Academy (SUA), Turner has served as its diversity director since 1998. She annually coordinates three schoolwide assemblies centering on diversity and inclusion of the school's LGBTQ, Asian, Latino and African American students. She conducts staff training on those same issues and co-organizes the ministry teams. Additionally, she annually leads the SUA Art Camp for sixth through eighth graders.

Turner sits on the boards of, among others, Cincinnati Preschool Promise, the Building Diverse Audiences Advisory Committee of the Aronoff Center for the Arts, and the Walnut Hills Redevelopment Foundation. In April 2019, the Cincinnati Symphony Orchestra presented Turner with its MAC (Multicultural Awareness Council) award for Diversity and Leadership in the Arts. The award recognizes those "who have forged paths for the inclusion of underrepresented communities in the arts."

Turner plans to simultaneously resuscitate her father's legacy and cement her own. She's received nonprofit certification for the Robert O'Neal Multicultural Arts Center to be located in either the West End or in Walnut Hills, and wants it built by 2021. "The Arts Consortium was such a hub. What's the next generation going to have? We've got to make that happen for them."

—Kathy Y. Wilson

SANDY UNDERWOOD

Sandy Underwood discovered a love for photography long before she owned a camera. Growing up in Lodi in north-central Ohio, she and her high school classmates traveled to Wooster to have their senior portraits taken.

She remembers staying behind to talk with the photographer, who offered her a job colorizing black-and-white portraits. "I watched him printing photos in the darkroom, then tried it myself, and then, 'Holy cow, here comes a picture!'" Underwood says. "I realized I could read light and knew the right exposures to use. It just came to me naturally."

She joined the Air Force after high school, mostly to get away and start a new life, but women's roles in the military were limited in the late 1950s. She took several tests to see "where I'd fit in," Underwood says, and, amazingly, was assigned to analyze photographs. She ended up training officers how to study spy photos at the War College at Maxwell Air Force Base in Alabama just as the U.S. space program was beginning. "They called me Sunny on the base," she says, "because I smiled whenever they yelled at me. It was better than crying."

After leaving the military, she visited Cincinnati to see friends and decided to stay, working as a photo lab tech before joining photographer Walt Burton's studio in Mt. Adams. "The darkroom in those days was the creative end of photography, learning what you could do with negatives to print just the right images," Underwood says. "Taking pictures was and still is an art, but so was the devel-oping work I did. And that's gone now with every-thing being digital."

Underwood would tag along on photo shoots with Burton, who had been hired by the then-new Play-house in the Park to document its shows. "Walt was an excellent photographer, but he wasn't good at show-ing up on time," she says. So she'd occasionally shoot the shows herself—and a new career was born.

The Playhouse hired Underwood on a one-year contract in 1973, which they renewed every sea-son over the next 40 years. She started shooting for Cincinnati Opera the same year, and eventually she would wind up documenting the city's growing performance-arts scene at Cincinnati Ballet, Cincin-nati Symphony, the May Festival, Ensemble Theatre Cincinnati, University of Cincinnati's College-Conser-vatory of Music, Cincinnati Shakespeare Company, and the School for Creative and Performing Arts.

Underwood officially retired in 2016, amassing what she estimates to be 1.5 million to 2 million im-ages of Cincinnati arts organizations throughout her career. "When I shot at the Playhouse and the Opera those first years, it was the first time in my life I felt like I had a home," she says. "I felt like I belonged in those arts organizations, that I was an artist too."

—John Fox

DIANA VANDERGRIFF-ADAMS

When Diana Vandergriff-Adams would travel to accompany Cincinnati Ballet and Cincinnati Opera costumes and sets on loan, she'd notice that many of the renting companies had stopped investing in quality workmanship on site.

They would build quick, cheap costumes for each show and then just throw them away after the run. "Costume-making has become more disposable, like a lot of things in this world," she says. "It's a dying art."

It's an art that Adams almost singlehandedly, with her own hands, kept alive for nearly 50 years at Music Hall. She officially retired from the Ballet in July 2019, a few seasons after departing the Opera, where she had also worked for 42 years. Her titles might have been different—she was Wardrobe Mistress at the Ballet and Costumer at the Opera—but Adams' role was similar: maker, repair expert, and keeper of the costumes; traveling ambassador tasked with getting expensive, one-of-a-kind costumes back home intact; and mother-away-from-home for many of the young, homesick performers who found themselves in Cincinnati. The foreign-born dancers, in particular, called her Mama Di.

Adams has a lot of favorite shows from across the decades, especially classic productions that allowed her to update and reuse vintage costumes already on hand. *Carmen*, which the Opera staged a number of times during her tenure, utilized costumes from the 1970s that Adams loved to tweak. For the Ballet's production of *Jewels*, she replicated choreographer George Balanchine's original costumes for the Rubies, Diamonds and Emeralds.

And she made 42 new tutus for *The Sleeping Beauty* in 2019, with each one taking between 80 and 120 hours to build by hand. The work was all worth it, though, when the curtain rose. "*The Sleeping Beauty* dancers would come on stage, and the audience always gasped," Adams says. "I loved hearing them go 'Ahhhh!'"

It wasn't always glamorous work, she admits, especially during the holidays for *The Nutcracker*, when she and her small staff would do nine loads of laundry after every performance. Or making those 42 new tutus by hand. Or working a nine-month Ballet season and immediately jumping into the Opera's summer season, with little downtime in between. But she's grateful that her artistic directors treasured production quality and attention to detail as much as she did.

As for her retirement, Adams says she has season tickets to both the Ballet and Opera, but otherwise she's trying to let go. "I miss the people, but I don't go into the backstage areas of Music Hall and visit. I don't want the current staff to feel like I'm judging them. I'm finished."

—John Fox

ANGELA POWELL WALKER

Born in Cincinnati, Angela Powell Walker grew up singing in her church and elementary school choir and plays. Those experiences would lay the foundation for her distinguished career—a journey that, in her own words, took "weird, winding paths."

She has amassed quite an array of titles: professional opera singer, beloved educator, producing artistic director. After graduating in 1986 from the Cincinnati Public Schools' School for Creative and Performing Arts (SCPA)—where she currently serves as artistic director—Powell Walker went on to attend Oberlin College, where she received a bachelor's degree in opera performance. It was there that she grew to love the craft. "I have a type of voice that is suited more toward the classical form," she said of deciding to study opera. "What most African-American women had to sing at the time, which is *Dreamgirls* and *Ain't Misbehavin'*, had that belchy kind of (sound). I'm not a belcher. And I was good at (opera)."

Powell Walker went on to obtain a master's degree in opera performance at the University of Maryland in 1994. During her operatic career, she has graced the stages of Cincinnati Opera, Dayton Opera, Kennedy Center for Performing Arts (where she also served as associate artistic director from 2005–2010), among others both nationally and internationally. Notably, she sang in and won the Metropolitan Opera Young Artist Competition in 1992. When asked what some of her favorite performing roles have been, she cited the title character in Carlisle Floyd's *Susannah* and the Countess in *The Marriage of Figaro*, the latter being a part she's played several times.

Her teaching career began in Washington D.C., where she taught out of her own private studio from 1994–2010. During that time, she also worked at Suitland High School (1994) and the prestigious Duke Ellington School of the Arts (2005-2010) before moving back to her hometown to serve as the first producing artistic director and chief executive officer of the Children's Theatre of Cincinnati. She was the first African-American woman in the role.

Moving back to Cincinnati partially stemmed from wanting to spend more time with her three sons and husband. Often traveling to perform, she felt that she was missing out on valuable time. "That's when I angled everything more toward education and coaching," she said. "I don't know how I became an arts administrator, but I am! And at my alma mater! I wouldn't do it for any other school, but at SCPA absolutely."

Powell Walker officially stepped into the role of SCPA's artistic director in 2015. And like the Children's Theatre, she became the school's first African-American woman in the role since its inception in 1973. It's a position of influence she is grateful that the community entrusts to her as she introduces students to the world of working in various arts-related fields.

Powell Walker sums up the breadth of her work and life the best: "I love what I do. I love the arts. I think that the arts are humanity. And that's just how I try to live my life every day."

—Mackenzie Manley

GINGER WARNER

Ginger Warner sees art everywhere she goes. She sees it in the rising sun, in a lovely chair, a tasteful lamp, and even in the subtle geometry of farmland. "Everything, if you look closely enough, is related to art," Warner said.

"The suit you wear, the design of a building, the music you hear—somebody used their artistic talents to make it happen."

Warner is a retired attorney and government relations specialist who may want to take another look at what retirement is supposed to mean. The list of organizations she has volunteered for, and boards she has served on, is almost impossibly long, including Cincinnati Symphony Orchestra, Seven Hills School, Ensemble Theatre Cincinnati, May Festival, Cincinnati Opera, and Taft Museum of Art.

But wait, there is more. Warner is a founder of The Harmony Project at the College-Conservatory of Music and has been on the Board of Trustees of the University of Cincinnati since 2012. She has been recognized by Caracole with their Living Award, by the Ohio Alliance for Arts Education for her commitment to the arts in Ohio, and by the *Cincinnati Enquirer* as a Woman of the Year.

Warner is also Chairman of the Ohio Arts Council, a state agency that funds art experiences to strengthen Ohio communities culturally, educationally, and economically. Warner loves the beauty of art, of course, but she is also a grinder. She will put in all the work needed to make that beauty happen. "Through art, the Council supports economic development, enriches schools, and can make a difference for everybody in the community," she said.

It is truly an extraordinary amount of work, but Warner is almost confused by the question of why she would do so much. "It is gratifying. It is so important. The arts can bring us together, and there are so many talented people who really just need the opportunity."

Nothing feels better for Warner than when a child is transformed by the arts, which is why she wants to make sure every child gets exposure to culture. She knows it can transform them, that an introduction to the arts is more than just taking in a show, seeing a play, or going to a museum.

"We changed the Council's programming. It is great to put a kid on the bus and take them to the symphony, but it is not enough," Warner said. "Now we do educational outreach. We go to the schools and prepare the students for what they are going to see and hear and experience. Then we take them to the symphony."

This type of commitment to children is part of why Warner has been honored so many times, even though she is not crazy about personal attention. Warner was given the William R. Joseph Ohio Arts Advocacy medal in 2016. At the time, Gary Hanson, former director of the Cleveland Orchestra, told the *Enquirer* that people appreciate Warner because she focuses on "substance rather than show. Much of her work is invisible, behind the scenes, but no one who meets her can doubt the passion of her commitment."

In truth, she is really just hoping to make a difference for children through the arts. "Oh my gosh, the excitement you see when their faces light up. You can see the sparkle in their eyes. And of course, they want more. So we will continue to provide more. It changes them."

—John Faherty

KATHY Y. WILSON

When I was eight years old, my third-grade teacher, Mrs. Tish, gave an assignment to interview an adult we admired. I chose Kathy. She's my sister. Not metaphorically. Genetically. We have the same mother and we're 12 years apart.

One of the questions I asked Kathy was, "Why do you read so much?" She answered, "I don't want my mind to turn into oatmeal." Mrs. Tish loved that response and I adored Mrs. Tish so her reaction to Kathy's wit confirmed my belief in Kathy's cleverness.

We were living in Denver, Colorado, at the time: Kathy, me, our mom, and my dad. During our time there, I fell in love with my big sister. My adoration often bordered on idolatry. Everything she said was hilarious and smart to me. (She even taught me the word, *hilarious*.) She let me borrow numerous cassettes *and* listen to them on *her* Walkman! She would take me to all these cool places like late shows at a movie theater and a record store that had its wares behind locked glass doors and used hypodermic needles littering its parking lot. But I always felt safe with Kathy. Safe and free. After we moved back to Cincinnati, Kathy and I would ride around in her stereo-less yellow 1970-something Volkswagen Beetle singing random songs at the top of our lungs or cracking jokes.

I didn't realize it at the time, but I was watching her find her way. Nowadays Kathy's known for her achievements (*Your Negro Tour Guide* column, book, and stage play) and accolades (Library Foundation Writer-in-Residence, Public Library of Cincinnati and Hamilton County; 2016 Sachs Fund Prize; 2018 University of Cincinnati Journalism Hall of Fame inductee).

But the road to those accomplishments was paved with exhaustive journal entries, comfortable but distracting jobs, private hells, and cathartic poetry.

Then one day, the poet became a journalist. My dad was a graphic designer at the *Journal-News* in Hamilton, Ohio—Kathy's birthplace and girlhood bedrock—when he encouraged her to pursue a writing opportunity with the newspaper. This was the springboard for Kathy's leap into a career that was pivotal to her development as a writer. The *Journal-News* is where Kathy began to hone her voice as a storyteller and, eventually, a columnist.

Kathy took me with her on an assignment she had to cover a Ku Klux Klan rally in Middletown, Ohio. It was the summer after my turbulent freshman year of college. Here we were again, going into dangerous territory together, but I still felt safe and free because I was with Kathy.

Hanging with my sister is still one of my favorite pastimes. I love rattling off my thoughts in her presence to see her reaction or hear her response (which is usually a guffaw of some sort). The older we get, the more we reminisce about our late mother or Denver memories. Oh, how I cherish these moments! I realize so many of my sentences still start with, "My sister Kathy…" because she's one of the co-authors of my life.

—Devin Parrish

WRITER BIOGRAPHIES

Dave Caudill, *freelance writer and journalist*
Former news and features editor for the *Cincinnati Enquirer*. Book and newsletter editor for the Episcopal Diocese of Southern Ohio.

Ray Cooklis, *journalist and editor*
Former classical music critic and editorial page editor for the *Cincinnati Enquirer*. Editor of *Movers and Makers* magazine.

Hillary Copsey, *freelance writer, editor and consultant*
Former director of communications & marketing at ArtsWave. Former reporter and editor for *Scripps Treasure Coast Newspapers* in Stuart, FL. Book advisor at Cincinnati's Mercantile Library.

Susan Fellows Crabtree, *marketing and branding*
Former brand and marketing executive in the financial services industry. Volunteer board member of arts organizations including Art Academy of Cincinnati and Cincinnati Ballet.

Mark Curnutte, *reporter, author, editor and faculty*
Faculty in Miami University's Department of Sociology and Gerontology. Former race and social justice reporter for the *Cincinnati Enquirer*. Author: *A Promise in Haiti: A Reporter's Notes on Families and Daily Lives* (2011) and *Across the Color Line: Reporting 25 Years in Black Cincinnati* (2019). Editor, "The State of Black Cincinnati: Two Cities" (2015).

Amy Miller Dehan, *curator and writer*
Curator of decorative arts and design at the Cincinnati Art Museum. Exhibit catalogues published in *The Magazine Antiques, Silver Magazine, Gastronomica*, and other periodicals.

John Faherty, *journalist and library director*
Former reporter for the *Cincinnati Enquirer*. Executive director of the Mercantile Library.

John Fox, *editor and writer*
Editor-in-chief of *Cincinnati Magazine*. Co-founder of *CityBeat*; editor and director of an events division (Cincinnati Entertainment Awards, MidPoint Music Festival). Editor of ArtWorks' *Transforming Cincinnati* 10th anniversary book.

Randy Freking, *author*
Partner at Freking Myers & Reul law firm. Author of *Cincinnati's 150 Year Opening Day History* (2018) and the "ABA Consumer Guide to Employee Rights" (2015).

Christi Geary, *freelance writer*
Director at the Bayer Company in digital marketing and innovation insights. Freelance writer focused on arts & humanities, travel, and children's stories.

Janelle Gelfand, *reporter and writer*
Lead arts writer for *Cincinnati Business Courier*. Former music and arts reporter for the *Cincinnati Enquirer*. Author of *Janelle's Notes*, a blog written for WGUC.

Brett Harper, *author and artist*
Son of artists Charley and Edith (Edie) Harper. Owner of the Charley and Edie Harper Art Studio. Co-author of *Harper Ever After: The Early Work of Charley and Edie Harper* (2015).

Dan Hurley, *historian, television producer, and author*
Founder of Applied History Associates. Historian and political reporter for WCPO and WKRC-TV. Former executive producer and host of Local 12 "Newsmakers." Author of five books including *Cincinnati: The Queen City*.

Joan Kaup, *editor*
Managing editor and publisher of *AAC 150: Make Art. Make a Difference*. Cincinnati: The Art Academy of Cincinnati, 2018.

Aiesha Little, *communications and freelance writer*
Freelance writer for *Soapbox Cincinnati, Ohio Magazine, Ghettoblaster* magazine, *Cincinnati Magazine, Columbus Monthly* magazine. Former writer for *The Detroit News* and *The Poughkeepsie Journal*.

Tiffany Luckey, *writer and editor*
Corporate communications for Ohio National Financial Services. Former associate editor for Custom Media (Akron) and *Writer's Digest* (Cincinnati, F+W), and former editorial assistant at the *Community Press* (Cincinnati).

David Lyman, *dance and theater critic, author*
Dance and theater critic, writer, editor, and copy writer for the *Cincinnati Enquirer*. Former arts writer and features editor for the *Detroit Free Press,* and film critic for the *Cincinnati Post*. Author of *Cincinnati Ballet Celebrates 50* (2013).

Mackenzie Manley, *writer and editor*
Arts and culture editor at *Cincinnati CityBeat*. Former editor-in-chief at *The Northerner,* Northern Kentucky University's student newspaper.

Kathy Merchant, *writer and editor*
Managing director and editor of *Cincinnati's Arts and the Power of Her*. Founder and author of Vino Ventures, an occasional wine blog, at kathymerchant.wine. Former president and CEO of Greater Cincinnati Foundation.

Carolyn Pione Micheli, *communications, writer and editor*
Vice president of corporate communications and investor relations for The E.W. Scripps Company. Former business editor for the *Cincinnati Enquirer*. Former managing editor for the *Baton Rouge Business Report*.

Constance Moore and Nancy Broermann, *authors*
Co-authors of *Maria Longworth Storer: From Music and Art to Popes and Presidents* (2019).

Devin K. Parrish, *author, playwright and freelance writer*
Senior editor at Scenario Learning. Playwright, director and producer of a one-act play. Author of *God's Favorite 21st Century Angel: A Collection of Memories*. Senior writer for CNN "Morning Express with Robin Meade" and "Weekend Express with Natasha Curry."

Rick Pender, *theater critic, journalist and author*
Assembled *The Stephen Sondheim Encyclopedia* (2019). Author of *100 Things To Do In Cincinnati Before You Die*, 1st and 2nd editions. Contributor to *CityBeat's* theater columns/reviews, and WVXU's "Around Cincinnati." Former executive editor and publisher of *Everything Sondheim*. Former arts and entertainment editor for *CityBeat*.

Erica Reid, *freelance writer*
Develops marketing strategies for orchestras and other arts organizations. Poet, theater critic, blog writer about adventures and art at *GoWestYoungWoman.com*. Former theater reviewer for *CityBeat*.

Steven Rosen, *reporter and freelance writer*
Contributing visual arts editor and arts writer for *CityBeat*. Freelance writer for various media including *The New York Times, Los Angeles Times, Variety,* indieWire.com, *Western Art & Architecture,* and *AmericanSongwriter*. Former *Denver Post* movie critic and reporter. Former reporter for *Cincinnati Enquirer*.

Maria Seda-Reeder, *writer, curator and lecturer*
Freelance writer covering living artists for various publications such as *Epicenter Magazine, Acrylic Artist, Pastel Journal, Watercolor Magazine,* and *Whitehot Magazine of Contemporary Art*. Adjunct instructor for University of Cincinnati's College of Design Architecture Art and Planning. Exhibition coordinator at Wave Pool Gallery.

Leyla Shokoohe, *freelance journalist*
Freelance journalist for *Cincinnati Business Courier, CityBeat,* and *Movers and Makers*. Former marketing and communications roles for Cincinnati Ballet, Cincinnati Symphony Orchestra, and ArtsWave.

Mary Stagaman, *freelance writer*
Vice president for inclusion at the Cincinnati USA Regional Chamber. Freelance writer for *Edible Ohio*. Former director of Agenda 360. Former leader of external relations and community engagement at University of Cincinnati.

Jeff Suess, *media librarian and author*
Librarian for *Enquirer* Media. Author: *Lost Cincinnati* (2015); *Hidden History of Cincinnati* (2016); and *Cincinnati Then and Now* (2018). Freelance copy editor for F+W Media.

Beth Sullebarger, *historic preservation consultant and author*
Author of *A Guide to Art and Architecture in Cincinnati's Parks*. Contributing author to *Architecture in Cincinnati: An Illustrated History of Designing and Building an American City*. President of the Stephen H. Wilder Foundation.

Ilene Ross Tucker, *writer and editor*
Founding editor of 513{eats}. Former senior dining writer for *CityBeat*.

Linda Vaccariello, *freelance writer and editor*
Former executive editor for *Cincinnati Magazine*. Former freelance writer for WGUC.

Kathy Y. Wilson, *freelance writer*
Freelance writer for *CityBeat* and *Cincinnati Magazine*. Library Foundation Writer-In-Residence at the Public Library of Cincinnati and Hamilton County. Awards: 2016 Sachs Fund Prize and 2018 University of Cincinnati Journalism Hall of Fame.

PHOTO APPENDIX

Thank you to the many contemporary women who provided favorite photos for use in this book. We applaud the many photographers, and thank so many contributors, whose shared images are credited here.

Chapter One

Georgia Beasley: Courtesy of University of Cincinnati archives.

Rosemary Clooney: *"Swing Around Rosie"* mural designed by Natalie Lanese, photo by J. Miles Wolf courtesy of ArtWorks.

Patricia Corbett: Singing with Jimmy James Orchestra, courtesy of Cincinnati Opera.

Doris Day: Singing in Cincinnati bandleader Barney Rapp's band, by William P. Gottlieb courtesy of Library of Congress and *Cincinnati Enquirer*.

Jackie Demaline: by Cara Owsley, courtesy of *Cincinnati Enquirer*.

Mary Emery: Portrait by Carolyn Schwenkmeyer, probably from a photo by Henry H. Pierce taken in 1910, courtesy of the Village of Mariemont.

Carol Ann Haile: provided by the Carol Ann and Ralph V. Haile, Jr. / U.S. Bank Foundation.

Edie McKee Harper: "Edie Self-Portrait," provided by Brett Harper.

Elizabeth "Betty" Wohlgemuth Herschede: with "John Z," by Ran Cochran courtesy of *Cincinnati Enquirer*.

Mary Ellyn Hutton: at Music Hall, provided by Elizabeth Hutton.

Irma Lazarus: by Mark Treitel, courtesy of *Cincinnati Enquirer*.

Ruth Lyons: courtesy of *Cincinnati Enquirer*.

Loretta Manggrum: Courtesy of University of Cincinnati archives.

Mary Louise McLaughlin: "Self Portrait at Age Sixty." Gouache and watercolor drawing. Gift of Theodore A. Langstroth, courtesy of Cincinnati Art Museum. Accession #1986.86.

Louise Nippert: by Patrick Reddy, courtesy of *Cincinnati Enquirer*.

Elizabeth Nourse: *"Self Portrait"* mural, photo by J. Miles Wolf courtesy of ArtWorks.

Harriet Marsh Page: at NKU, by Fred Straub courtesy of *Cincinnati Enquirer*.

Norma Petersen: *Enquirer* Woman of the Year 2000, by Tony Jones courtesy of *Cincinnati Enquirer*.

Patricia Renick: by Laura Chapman, courtesy of *Cincinnati Magazine*.

Mamie Smith: *"Dreaming Blues"* mural, photo by J. Miles Wolf courtesy of ArtWorks.

Harriet Beecher Stowe: by Fisher Alanson, Smithsonian National Portrait Gallery; courtesy of *Cincinnati Enquirer*.

Aralee Strange: by Fred Straub, courtesy of *Cincinnati Enquirer*.

Anna Sinton Taft: Portrait by Raimundo de Madrazo y Garreta. Oil on canvas; 49 1/2 x 38 1/8 in. (125.1 x 96.84 cm). Bequest of Charles Phelps Taft and Anna Sinton Taft, courtesy of Taft Museum of Art, Cincinnati, Ohio. [4.1931]

Alice Weston: provided by Jim Rauth.

Phyllis Weston: Great Living Cincinnatian 2013, courtesy of Cincinnati USA Regional Chamber.

Chapter Two

Sarah Worthington King Peter: 1854 Marble bust by Charles H. Bullett (American, b.1824, d.1873), sculptor. Gift of Mrs. Rufus King, courtesy of Cincinnati Art Museum. [1896.4]

Paige Williams: by @tannerbrown, provided.

Elizabeth Williams Perry: Portrait by Henry Pierce (1864-1943), platinum print. Courtesy of Cincinnati Art Museum, Library Transfer. [1981.278]

Mary Johnston: courtesy of Cincinnati Art Museum.

Alice Bimel: by Tom Hubbard, courtesy of *Cincinnati Enquirer*; reproduced from the collection of the Mary R. Schiff Library & Archives, Cincinnati Art Museum.

Anita J. Ellis: by Erin Geideman, provided.

Tamara Harkavy: by Peggy Joseph Photography, provided.

Margaretta Baker-Hunt: courtesy of Kenton County Public Library archives.

Myrl Laurence et al: L-R: Myrl Laurence, Dorothy Potts, Rita O'Neill, Virginia Garrett and Nancy Bauer; by Mayhew Photographers, courtesy of *Cincinnati Enquirer*.

Victoria Morgan: by Jennifer Denham, provided.

Jennifer Archibald: by Anders J. Larsson, provided.

Heather Britt: by Sarah Laubacher, provided.

Kathy DeLaura: by Erica Milligan, provided.

Blanche Maier: L-R Victoria Morgan, Blanche Maier, provided by Karen Maier.

Arlene Gibeau: courtesy of Kenton County Public Library archives.

Sara Vance Waddell: by Helen Adams Photography, provided.

Litsa Spanos: by Hudson Carmel, provided.

Robyn Reeves Lana: by Lynn Siegfried, provided.

Clara Baur: courtesy of *Cincinnati Enquirer*.

Bertha Baur: by Albert Kuprion, courtesy of *Cincinnati Enquirer*.

Peggy Crawford et al: L-R: Betty Pollak Rauh, Peggy Frank Crawford, and Rita Rentschler Cushman; courtesy of Contemporary Arts Center.

Raphaela Platow: by Tina Gutierrez, provided.

Zaha Hadid: by Michael Keating, courtesy of *Cincinnati Enquirer*.

Jefferson James: *"Park Dance"* by Sandy Underwood, provided.

Ruth Sawyer and Mary "Murph" Mahler: courtesy of Ensemble Theatre Cincinnati.

D. Lynn Meyers: by Mikki Schaffner, provided.

Carolyn Wallace: by Nina Wells, provided.

Lydia Morgan: by Leigh Taylor, courtesy of *Cincinnati Enquirer*.

Junior League: Docent Mary Lou Richardson, courtesy of Mary R. Schiff Library and Archives, Cincinnati Art Museum.

Maria Longworth Storer: courtesy of The American Ceramic Society, provided.

Catherine Roma: "CincySings at the World Choir Games" by Phil Groshong, provided.

Elizabeth Weicher Pierce: courtesy of Cincinnati Museum Center.

Francie Hiltz: by Steven Easley

Patricia K. Beggs: painting by Polish artist Rafał Olbiński that became the poster for *Tosca*, courtesy of Cincinnati Opera.

Lois Rosenthal: by Tony Jones, courtesy of *Cincinnati Enquirer*.

Ellen van der Horst: "Spirit of Cincinnati USA Champion Award, Cincinnati Convention & Visitors Bureau," provided.

Marni Penning: by Sarah Case, provided.

Helen Louise "Nellie" Herron Taft: photo by Harris & Ewing, courtesy of Library of Congress, Prints & Photographs Division. [LC-USZ62-25804]

Mary Judge: courtesy of Cincinnati Symphony Orchestra.

Sue Friedlander: "Greater Cincinnati Foundation Annual Report," courtesy of Mary Strubbe.

Deborah Emont Scott: courtesy of the Taft Museum of Art.

Vernita Henderson: courtesy of the Taft Museum of Art.

Sallie Robinson Wadsworth: courtesy of the Taft Museum of Art.

Woman's Art Club: *"Emerge"* mural designed by Tina Westercamp; photo by J. Miles Wolf courtesy of ArtWorks.

Women's Alliance: "Youth Empowerment." L-R Carole Hawkins, Nicole Dowdell, Former CPS Superintendent Mary Ronan, Mary Gaither Smith, Carol Rigaud; provided.

Chapter Three

Sandra Vazquez and Raquel Guillen: by Hector Ariza, provided.

Dianne Dunkelman: by Janine Spring, provided.

Ixi Chen: by Jake Anderson, provided.

Anupama Mirle: by Santosh Gidadmani, provided.

Siri Imani: *"Look Around"* courtesy of Cincinnati Symphony Orchestra.

Calcagno Cullen: by Mark Curnutte.

Chapter Four

Shannon Carter: Great Living Cincinnatian, provided.

Alva Jean Crawford: Great Living Cincinnatian, courtesy of Cincinnati USA Regional Chamber.

Kathryne Gardette: by Michael D. Price/Fairfield Photography, provided.

Janelle Gelfand: by Paula Norton, courtesy of *Cincinnati Business Courier*.

Nikki Giovanni: by Deborah Feingold, provided.

Amy Goodwin: by Angie Lipscomb, provided.

Robin Guarino: by J. Henry Fair, provided.

Heather Hallenberg: by Helen Adams Photography, provided.

Pam Kravetz: by annettenavarro.com, courtesy of *Cincinnati Magazine*.

Quiera Levy-Smith: by Kate Messer, courtesy of *Cincinnati Enquirer*.

Rhoda Mayerson: by Annie Leibovitz, provided.

Constance McClure: portrait by student Katelyn Wolary, courtesy of Art Academy of Cincinnati.

Mary McCullough-Hudson: by Tina Gutierrez, provided.

Ellen Muse-Lindeman: by Will Jones, provided.

Annie Ruth: by Shellee Fisher, provided.

Melody Sawyer Richardson: by Claudia Hershner, courtesy of Cincinnati Symphony Orchestra.

Ann Santen: courtesy of Greater Cincinnati Foundation.

Rosemary Schlachter: by Mark Schlachter, provided.

Kristen Schlotman: filming "The Public," courtesy of Brian Douglas.

Reba Senske: courtesy of *Cincinnati Business Courier*.

Marie Speziale: courtesy of Rice University, provided.

Toilynn O'Neal Turner: courtesy of Cincinnati Symphony Orchestra.

Diana Vandergriff-Adams: courtesy of *Cincinnati Magazine*.

Ginger Warner: *Enquirer* Woman of the Year, by Ernest Coleman courtesy of *Cincinnati Enquirer*.

Kathy Y. Wilson: by Tony Walsh, provided.